Ready, Launch, Brand

Ready, Launch, Brand
The Lean Marketing Guide for Startups

By Orly Zeewy

"Action without vision is a dream.
Vision without action is a nightmare."
Japanese Proverb

Routledge
Taylor & Francis Group

A PRODUCTIVITY PRESS BOOK

First published 2021
by Routledge
600 Broken Sound Parkway #300, Boca Raton FL, 33487

and by Routledge
2 Park Square, Milton Park, Abingdon, Oxon, OX14 4RN

Routledge is an imprint of the Taylor & Francis Group, an informa business

ISBN: 978-0-367-46718-0 (hbk)
ISBN: 978-0-367-46662-6 (pbk)
ISBN: 978-1-003-03060-7 (ebk)

Typeset in Minion
by SPi Global, India

This book is dedicated to my two favorite startups, my sons Jake and Sam.

Contents

Acknowledgments

Many people supported me on the way to getting this book published. My patient and gifted editor, Louis Greenstein helped me wrestle my book into a cohesive narrative. Jamie Bischoff, Esq., provided invaluable legal advice, editing direction, and encouragement. Ann de Forest helped me craft my book proposal. Rob Fleming was an early advocate and recommended my book to his publisher. Franne McNeal provided much-needed professional and publishing advice. Miriam Seidel provided the cover art. Christian Sarkar, editor of *The Marketing Journal*, encouraged me to write the blogposts which form the backbone of this book.

I want to thank my colleagues, friends, and family who believed in this book and encouraged me during this long journey—and especially my dad, who gifted me with the love of entrepreneurship and has been my biggest champion.

Finally, I'd like to thank the entrepreneurs who are featured in this book: Nick Bayer, Ethan Bresnahan, Joe and Lily Born, Anthony Gold, Alexis Lieberman, Bob Maiden, Nancy MacIntyre, Jay Minkoff, RJ Napolitano, and Brynne Tillman. Thank you for sharing your time, your advice, and your stories.

Introduction: Are You Ready to Take Over the World?

There's lots of bad reasons to start a company. But there's only one good, legitimate reason, and I think you know what it is: it's to change the world.

—**Phil Libin,** CEO, Evernote

Startups move at the speed of light, and time to market is critical. According to author Steve Blank, aka the father of modern entrepreneurship, "a scalable startup founder doesn't just want to be her own boss; she wants to take over the universe. From day one her intent is to grow her startup into a large, disruptive company."

Entrepreneurs, who are overwhelmed getting their startups off the ground, typically relegate marketing to "when I'm ready and can afford it" status. But there's a problem: Unless marketing is integrated into the DNA of your startup culture, there will never be money to spend on it. The question that founders should be asking is not "When will we be ready for marketing?" but "What should we do now so we'll be ready when it's time to scale our business?"

Traditional marketing is expected and necessary for established companies. Without it, customers might wonder if those companies are still in business. But for startups, ads, billboards, bus shelters, and other traditional marketing buys are not only expensive, but they don't work. That's because startups don't have a proven track record to build on, and most are still trying to figure out who they are. It's hard to sell something that you yourself aren't clear on.

Steve Blank reminds us that: "Startups are not just a smaller version of a larger company" but an entirely new kind of system. A traditional business plan, he says, will be obsolete within six months—and so will a traditional marketing plan.

Traditional marketing assumes that you're already familiar with the company and its brand. It builds on a brand's reputation and reminds customers of the benefits they've come to expect over a period of years. Startups aren't interested in the status quo. Many are looking to disrupt not just an industry, but an entire ecosystem.

In 2001, Apple didn't just launch the iPod. They created a new way of listening to music. And in 2008 they introduced us to the App Store. From the start, they have stayed on message with bold graphics and sleek products that engender FOMO—the fear of missing out, a trend identified in 2000 by marketing strategist Dan Herman.

Startups need to get clear on their value proposition from the start because all too often, "later" is late. To scale quickly, they need to understand what motivates early adopters to buy their product, instead of sticking with what they already have. Steve Jobs built his startup on a clear and memorable brand promise: Think Different. The tagline, created by the advertising firm TBWA/Chiat/Day in 1997, became a rallying cry for Apple's turnaround. More than twenty years later, Apple stays true to that promise. Instead of focusing on how the MacBook Pro (2006) or the iPad (2010) works, they show us the possibilities of what we can do with the technology. They still dare us to *think different*. That's one of the reasons that Apple has become the go-to of creatives worldwide.

This book provides the Lean Marketing guide that startups need if they are to build critical brand awareness now. I'll address seven startup marketing myths and provide a practical roadmap to building a successful Lean Marketing plan from the start of your business. And I'll share first-person marketing stories from founders who survived many false starts in building their brand. Each one will share their experiences, their lessons learned, and their advice for startups. In addition, I will introduce some key trends that are shaping entrepreneurs and today's startup culture.

So, let's brand!

1

If You Ask the Wrong Question, the Answer Doesn't Matter

Marketing Myth #1: Marketing is just smoke and mirrors.

> *Marketing and branding are some of the most important early-stage indicators of a company's potential success.*
>
> —**Mamoon Hamid**, venture capitalist and partner, Kleiner Perkins

WHO ARE YOU?

Are you an elephant or an alligator? Because, let's face it: if you're an alligator, then why are you planting shrubs and grassland instead of creating wetlands? All too often, founders expect marketing to be a magic pill that fixes vague messaging and the lack of a clear value proposition. Yet, they never even ask themselves the essential questions. How are we different from our competition? Are we clear on our ideal target customer, and, more important, do we know what matters to them? If we don't know, what do we need to do to find out? If you can't answer these questions, no amount of marketing will help you increase sales. This is the "closed loop" of marketing. If you expect marketing to fail, you won't look for answers; you'll keep doing the same thing, guaranteeing that marketing will fail.

With traditional marketing, the goal is growing an existing business, but Lean Marketing helps startups get clear on who they think they are as a brand and who they are trying to connect with (ideal customers). Lean Marketing takes the guesswork out of marketing in that critical first year so your startup can build brand awareness more quickly with the right customer. And just like traditional marketing, it's a process with clear metrics so founders know when their goals have been met.

FOUNDER STORY: ANTHONY GOLD, ROAR FOR GOOD

ROAR for Good is a mission-driven technology company dedicated to cultivating safer workplaces. Their platform, AlwaysOn, was designed to protect hotel employees.

When I founded my first startup in 2012, we thought of marketing as a transitional moment, so we did it all wrong. When we started ROAR for Good in 2015, a smart, safety wearable device for women, we wanted to make sure we were building something that the market would buy. We didn't want confirming data; we didn't want to know whether or not people liked it. We sat in coffee shops with pictures of our prototype and asked people why it wouldn't work. We spoke with dozens of people over a period of a couple of months and sent out surveys using Facebook and Google forms, targeting women, and conducted a random drawing for a gift card to incentivize people to talk to us. We collected hundreds of data points, from self-defense group instructors and women who wanted to learn about self-defense. What we learned shattered our initial hypothesis that women want a self-defense tool, but the problem is that it's hard to get to. At the time, we considered a mace bracelet that would shoot out pepper spray and spent time on engineering it. What we found out is that mace is illegal in several states, and women are frightened by self-defense tools and the idea of being overpowered. Our research led to a brand-new framework. We went back to our mission, which is to end rape and reduce the murder rate for women.

We thought we had a brilliant idea and that women would love it. They hated it. The sooner you're able to show it's a bad idea, the less time you spend investing in something that will fail.

—**Anthony Gold**, co-founder and COO, ROAR for Good

Advice to Founders

Many entrepreneurs have a great idea. As a serial entrepreneur, I've found that, typically, you are either solving a major pain point or addressing an opportunity. It's all in the execution. I've seen medio-cre ideas succeed because of how well they were executed. You also have to be open to pivot on a dime when your research shows you are wrong. Some of the best products have come out of failure. Look for a market opportunity and be prepared to be surprised.

THE ODDS OF STARTUP SUCCESS

More than 500,000 companies are launched every month in the United States alone. Eight out of ten will fail in the first five years. Three key factors account for this sobering trend. Number one is that there is no market need for what they offer. The other two reasons? Startups run out of cash, and they don't have the right team.

If you want your startup to beat those tough odds, you'll need to invest enough time to research your market, identify and verify your revenue model, and develop a viable strategy for how you'll reach your customers. Remember that consumer products are the most expensive and time-consuming to launch because your marketing will have to cover a lot of media channels to get a consumer's attention. What startups fail to consider is that new products are just that—new. You'll have to earn consumers' trust while you educate them on why your product is better than what they already use. Social media is a great way to shorten that cycle. If you can tap into key influencers with 100,000+ followers who love your product, they can help get your name out and build your brand awareness more quickly than you can on your own. But social media can be a double-edged sword. One wrong move, and 100,000+ consumers won't be shy about telling everyone in their network.

As a startup, building the right team is critical to scaling your business. But too often, founders come together on the basis of a vague concept of a future success rather than on shared values. It's much easier to build the right team when you can quickly recognize when someone is a fit with your brand's values and when they're not. This is why clarifying your brand's value proposition is so important from the start. Do you know

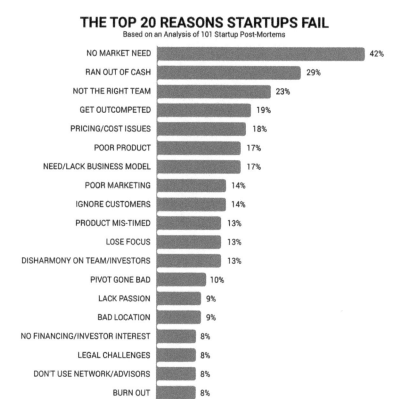

FIGURE 1.1
Top 20 Reasons that Startups Fail

what makes your brand different? Do you have a core value that will grow with you? Are you willing to build an entire company on that core value?

Nordstrom empowers its employees to accept any return, even when it's merchandise they don't sell. Nordstrom lore offers many examples, such as the time in the mid-1970s when the department store chain purchased a tire store in Fairbanks, Alaska, and turned it into a men's store. One day, a confused shopper brought a set of tires into the store asking for a refund, and without missing a beat, the salesperson took them back without a receipt, no questions asked—even though Nordstrom has never sold tires. That's what customer service looks like when it's at the heart of your business.

DO YOU HAVE AN UGLY BABY?

Once you've completed your market research, take the time to understand who your ideal customer is, what that customer wants, and, most important, if they are willing to pay for your product or service. You'll need to talk to a lot of people to make sure you've targeted the right customers and your product addresses a true pain point or problem. You may find that people have come up with a workaround that renders your product obsolete, but with additional data, you might just create a more viable, affordable, and attractive product that leaves their workaround in the dust. Or, you could learn of a more pressing problem that your customer is struggling with, one that your product could easily address.

Finally, before you invest in launching a new product or service, ask yourself: Are there enough people with the same problem to make my business viable? Your family and ten of your closest friends is not a market share. That's why it's so important to talk to people you don't know and who have no vested interest in your success. You'll gain much better insights, and you'll avoid confirmation bias.

Instead of launching a market-ready product or service and looking for a problem to solve, take a page from *The Startup Owner's Manual* by Steve Blank. Identify who you believe will be your potential customer—your early adopters. Create a minimum viable product (MVP) and "get out of the building" and listen to what they have to say about it. Be prepared to hear that you have an ugly baby. Don't ask if they like it. It doesn't matter if they do. Ask tough, open-ended questions and be willing to make changes. Don't assume that your MVP is the only prototype you'll ever build. Instead, ask what's missing; if they would do anything differently and why. When people call your baby ugly, ask them what you can do to make it beautiful.

> *There is nothing wrong in change, if it is in the right direction. To improve is to change, so to be perfect is to have changed often.*
>
> —Winston Churchill

THE RIGHT PRODUCT; THE WRONG CUSTOMER

Have you ever wondered how bubble wrap would look on your walls? In the 1950s, wallpaper was all the rage in American homes. In 1957, American engineer Alfred W. Fielding and Swiss inventor Marc Chavannes set out to create a brand-new product: textured wallpaper. Their first prototype, or minimum viable product (MVP), consisted of two shower curtains sealed together in such a way that it created air bubbles, giving the wallpaper a textured appearance. A new decorating idea was born. Sadly, it turned out that nobody wanted plastic sheets with air bubbles on their walls. Great product, wrong customer.

When they heard that they'd created an ugly baby, Fielding and Chavannes didn't give up. Instead of trying to convince decorators and homeowners to buy their textured wallpaper (and wasting a lot of marketing dollars trying to change their minds), they set aside their personal feelings and asked the right question: Where else might this product work? They tried to market their product as greenhouse insulation, but also without success. And then one day they stumbled on the perfect market fit. Shipping.

FIGURE 1.2
Bubble Wrap Wallpaper

From its inception, Bubble Wrap® was both a product and a value proposition. It could reduce total packaging cost by using less material, reduce package size and weight, and reduce loss from damage. It promoted sustainability long before it was fashionable. Sealed Air, the company that produces Bubble Wrap®, even established labs known as Package Design and Development Centers to educate their sales force about shock and vibration protection. To this day, it continues to work with customers to improve on their offerings.

Entrepreneurs are by their very nature disruptors, and history is full of ingenious and groundbreaking ideas that have changed the way we work and live. Apps are now so ubiquitous that it's easy to forget that they've only been around for a decade. The iPod didn't just change the way we listen to music; it revolutionized the music industry.

Before you start, do your best to fail so you won't invest a lot of money and time on the wrong product or service, for the wrong customer. Do your research and remember to ask potential customers what problems they really need solving, or you may end up with a lot of textured wallpaper on your hands.

We'll wrap up this chapter with an exercise to help you identify your brand's core value.

CORE VALUE EXERCISE

1. Write the first three words that come to mind when you think of your brand.
2. Put the words in order of importance.
3. Make a list of related words under each of your three words.
4. The one with the most words under it is your core value.

2

The Nike Syndrome

Marketing Myth #2: We'll pay for marketing when we can afford it.

> *In a crowded marketplace, fitting in is a failure.*
> *In a busy marketplace, not standing out*
> *is the same as being invisible.*
>
> —**Seth Godin**, author

Roughly half a million people become entrepreneurs every month in the U.S. alone.[1] According to the U.S. Bureau of Labor Statistics (BLS), 20% of startups fail during the first two years, 45% during the first five years, and 65% during the first ten years.

> ## 45% of startups fail
> during the first five years of business.
>
> (U.S. Business Bureau of Labor Statistics, 2020)[1]

You want your company to be among the ones to beat the odds, to be the 55% that make it to year five and beyond. Marketing—from day one—is critical to the rapid growth you need to beat those odds. But unless marketing is integrated into a startup's DNA today, chances are there won't be money in the budget for marketing tomorrow.

> *We never had a strategic sales plan for marketing.*
> *When it came down to hiring a programmer*
> *or spending money on marketing, we hired the*
> *programmer because we viewed them as critical to our*
> *business. The marketing we did do was "Helter Skelter"*
> *and as a result, we weren't as successful as we could*
> *have been and eventually closed the business.*
>
> —**Bob Maiden**, founder, The Maxwell Group

FOUNDER STORY: JAY MINKOFF, FIRST FLAVOR

First Flavor was founded to disrupt the food industry with an edible strip and product taste sampler.

In the early days of First Flavor, we spent a lot of money creating a logo and developing marketing collateral, but we didn't invest enough money in market research to identify our target market. You have to shape your collateral based on the problem you are solving for the right customer. Instead, we created collateral and then looked for our customer. We ran focus groups with consumers who loved our product. What we didn't do was conduct research with food and marketing executives, who turned out to be our real customers. We should have done focus groups with them so we could fully understand the decision makers in their sales cycle. We didn't ask how our product changed the opportunities for our target market, and it turns out that understanding the customer is always key. This is Marketing 101: you need to focus on the cost of acquisition and understand your Energy Return on Investment (EROI), or the cost of acquiring a customer.

> *Learn how to think differently about marketing, not just how to do it.*
>
> —**Jay Minkoff**, founder and former CEO, First Flavor

The three most successful things we did, and that I'm the proudest of:

- Getting a half-page article in the *Wall Street Journal* to highlight the flavor of Welch's Grape Juice.
- Getting an ad insert in *People* magazine—the first flavored ad in history.
- Appearing live on the *Today* show and Al Roker commenting on funny potential flavors for our taste strips.

Advice to Founders

Don't spend any money on marketing until you're sure you understand what you're building, and have a clear understanding of who your customer is and what matters to that customer. It took us nearly five years and a couple million dollars to figure out that we should have focused on companies that sampled their products and introduced First Flavor as an accurate and innovative way to do that. Instead, we focused on trying to sell the guy responsible for national grocery chains like ACME.

Epilogue

First Flavor was founded in 2005 and closed in 2013.

Market research is one area that most startups either don't invest in or don't understand the importance of.

—**Jay Minkoff**, founder and former CEO, First Flavor

WE'RE NOT NIKE

I've helped dozens of entrepreneurs and business owners build the DNA of their brands, and in the process, I've identified a phenomenon I call the "Nike Syndrome." When deciding whether to spend money on marketing, entrepreneurs often cite Nike as the reason it will never work.

The script goes something like this: "Of course it's easy to market when you're Nike. They are the #1 sports brand in the world and have deep pockets. I'm just a little company." The marketing myth is that a startup has to wait years before it will be able to spend money on traditional marketing and that there are no options for them at the start of their business. This narrow view keeps startups from growing fast—and reinforces the paradigm that marketing is only for big companies. What founders fail to recognize is that Nike was not always "Nike."

Back in January 1964, Nike was a young startup known as Blue Ribbon Sports (BRS), the brainchild of University of Oregon track athlete Philip Knight and his coach Bill Bowerman. Geoff Hollister, another teammate, joined as co-founder in those early years.

So how did little BRS become the mega brand known today as Nike? From the start, the founders had a clear vision: to provide the best running shoes for competitive athletes. After all, they were athletes themselves, so they had a unique perspective and a core understanding of their target customer. As a result, they were passionate about educating people on the benefits of running. Since BRS didn't have a lot of money for marketing, the founders did something quite unusual for the times. They asked college basketball players to wear their shoes and give them feedback on their performance. As those college players became professional players, the BRS reputation for exceptional basketball shoes grew with them. As a result, BRS built a base of "Brandvangelists," one enthusiastic fan at a time. Today, that fan base has grown to include Olympic athletes and the most recognized names in sports.

A common side effect of the "Nike Syndrome" is the reluctance of most business owners to consider changing their company's name, even when it fails to connect with customers and limits their growth and success. BRS was no different. Blue ribbons are meaningful in county fairs, but they don't carry the same gravitas in a growing global company; it took BRS fourteen years to recognize the limitation of their name and change it to Nike. In 1987 Nike hired Scott Bedbury "to turn around the struggling #3 athletic footwear brand."[2] Bedbury, who was Nike's advertising director from 1987 to 1994, spearheaded the "Just Do It" campaign and helped position the company as the #1 sports brand in the world, where it's been ever since.

IT TOOK NIKE NEARLY TWENTY YEARS TO BECOME NIKE

In 2019, Nike was valued at roughly $34.4 billion and their marketing budget was nearly $3.8 billion. It is a generally accepted rule of thumb that companies should spend 5% of total revenue on marketing to maintain their current position. If you're looking to grow or gain a larger market share, you should double your marketing budget, or 10% of total revenue. In highly competitive industries—retail, consumer products, and pharmaceuticals—that number can run from 20% to 50%.[3] Startups should expect to spend around 15%. In the early days of a startup, it's all about building brand awareness and brand loyalty, and doing that takes time and resources. Finding customers for your product is great, but if you don't build brand advocates from the start, it will be harder to scale up later. This line of thinking is at the core of Lean Marketing.

Effective marketing is scalable, which means you need to consider where you are in your business cycle and remember that "one size does not fit all." Successful companies recognize the value of marketing and treat it like a capital investment (instead of an item on their balance sheet). They have a reasonable marketing budget and spend more, not less, when business is going well, because in lean economic times, companies that have invested in marketing do better than the ones that don't (Figure 2.1).

A key component of Lean Marketing is getting clear on your startup's value proposition. I find that many founders don't take the time to identify their value proposition. This puts them at a distinct disadvantage when they try to convert prospects into customers. It's part of the "we'll get to that later" mindset. So, what is a value proposition? According to Peep Laja, founder of CXL, a value proposition is a clear statement that:

- Explains how your product solves customers' problems or improves their situation
- Delivers specific benefits
- Tells the ideal customer why they should buy from you and not from the competition

At its core, a value proposition is your brand's promise of the value it will deliver to your customers.[4]

When you don't have a value proposition, it's harder to identify marketing opportunities at the start of the business; marketing's status is relegated to

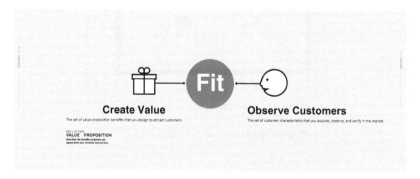

FIGURE 2.1
Value Proposition Map

either "do nothing until we can afford it" or "put a little money in traditional advertising and see what happens." Each is a recipe for failure. The problem with spending a little on advertising is that it doesn't work. Mega brands spend millions on advertising because if they didn't, people would forget they were a mega brand. According to Jeffry Pilcher, CEO and founder of The Financial Brand, research has shown that messages are more effective when repeated. Most marketing experts, he says, believe that messaging should follow the "Rule of 7:" A consumer must be exposed to an advertising message seven times before they remember it. And that's just the start. Nike's iconic tagline, "Just Do It" was first used in 1988. Nike has invested millions of dollars over three decades to make their tagline stick in consumers' minds.

The average startup doesn't have the resources to follow the "Rule of 7." And when their attempts don't yield quick results, they fall back on their confirmation bias, which tells them that marketing doesn't work.

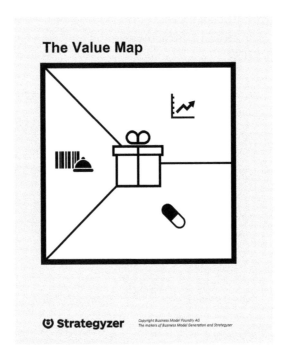

FIGURE 2.2
Value Map Building Blocks: Product/Service, Competitive Advantage, Reduce Customer Pain

Companies that market the way Nike did back when it was Blue Ribbon might not dominate an industry like Nike, but they'll be in that 55%.

We'll wrap up this chapter with an exercise to help you identify your business's unique value proposition (Figure 2.2).

VALUE PROPOSITION EXERCISE

Answer the following questions:

1. What is your product or service? (tech app, financial consulting, etc.).
2. How does your product/service help your ideal customer reduce a major pain point or provide a tangible gain they couldn't achieve without you? (better, faster, more easily than what they are using/doing now).
3. My product/service is unlike the competition because … (In what ways?)

Now look at your answers and write your value proposition: Our product/service is the only _____ that _____.

Congratulations! You know your value proposition.

NOTES

1 https://learn.g2.com/small-business-statistics
2 Scott Bedbury, *A New Brand World* (New York and London: Viking, 2002).
3 https://www.frog-dog.com/how-much-should-companies-budget-for-marketing
4 https://cxl.com/blog/value-proposition-examples-how-to-create/

3

The Gold Standard

Word-of-Mouth

Marketing Myth #3: We don't need marketing because all our business comes from referrals.

More startups fail from a lack of customers than from a failure of product development. What we need are processes to gain, keep, and grow our customer relationships.

—**Steve Blank**, father of modern entrepreneurship

Founders typically point to word-of-mouth as the Holy Grail of success. From their perspective, they don't need marketing because they already get great referrals. The thing is, when you truly understand who you're trying to target and why they should want what you're selling, it becomes much easier to attract and keep the right customers. It also means you start getting better and more qualified leads, which helps build brand evangelists—the true Holy Grail of marketing.

FOUNDER STORY: ALEXIS LIEBERMAN, MD, FAIRMOUNT PEDIATRICS

Fairmount Pediatrics was established in 2009 in the Fairmount area of Philadelphia.

In April 2009, I learned from another pediatrician about the stroller explosion going on in the Fairmount area of Philadelphia. Before I opened my practice, I researched both the location for my practice and what my future patients would want in a pediatrician. I walked around the neighborhood and spoke with moms walking their dogs and pushing strollers. I eventually found out who the five people were in the neighborhood who were movers and shakers and reached out to them. I set up a coffee meet-and-greet at a local coffee shop and met with more than seventy-five people over a period of three months. And I learned a lot! Moms told me that kids get restless, so a blackboard at their level would make it easier for them to wait. They told me what kinds of books their kids loved. I went to people's homes and met with families, so by the time I opened my practice, those families already knew me and trusted me. I opened my practice on September 10, 2009, and by then I already had thirty patients.

Parents were the customers but their children were the patients, so I had to gain the trust of both.

—**Alexis Lieberman**, MD, founder, Fairmount Pediatrics

Instead of jumping in and hoping to get customers, I learned a lot by talking with potential families. I found that face-to-face meetings were the best way to learn what my future patients wanted and set up my practice based on their input and recommendations. I learned that the parents were the customers but the children were the patients, so I had to gain the trust of both. Because I was an unknown in the neighborhood, the couple talks I tried at Whole Foods failed to gain traction, and because I was not in control of the promotion, only a couple of people showed up. I thought that nurses would be good referral sources for me, but it turned out that their patients already had a pediatrician and would not switch based on the nurse's recommendation.

Because my time was not as valuable in the beginning, I could afford to take the time to meet with moms and families. This turned out to be the most important marketing I did. It helped me build awareness for my brand and created a relaxed setting to hear stories and show my bedside manner. Kids responded well to me, as did their parents. The best lesson I learned was to identify who my ideal patients, and customers, were and go talk to them. Because my patients are children, it was critical to engage with their parents because they needed to feel comfortable with the doctor that their children were going to see.

I loved meeting with the moms and getting firsthand information that I could put to use in my new practice. We've had a blackboard at toddler height from the start. We've had a library of books that came from the recommendations that parents made. Being able to get that kind of information from the very people I wanted to come in as patients was invaluable. It also showed me the kind of practice I wanted. One where I could spend quality time with each of my patients and their families.

Advice to Founders

Do your research and remember to identify who you think will be your customers and talk to them. Find out what matters to them and follow their advice whenever possible.

Epilogue

Fairmount Pediatrics is listed among the top ten pediatric practices in Philadelphia and has grown into a holistic practice that includes adolescents. Fairmount Pediatrics and Adolescent Medicine includes a physical therapist, a speech therapist, a behavioral therapist, a homeopath, a psychologist, a lactation counselor, a nutritionist, and a craniosacral therapist.

Your brand is what other people say about you when you're not in the room.

—**Jeff Bezos**, *CEO, Amazon*

GETTING READY FOR GROWTH

One of the key stumbling blocks to growth is that without a well-defined brand, a startup can't build a sustainable company culture. Then, when the time comes to grow, it's difficult to attract top talent. Understanding who you are as a brand and who you are not is part of the early days of brand building. But all too often, founders skip this essential step and start selling (marketing) before they've identified their value proposition, their competitive advantage, their ideal customer, and why it matters to that customer.

So, where do you begin the process of building a brand when you're a startup? Most founders believe their companies will build their culture and their customer base as they scale, and that marketing is something they will get to when "they can afford it." In the previous chapter, I noted the importance of identifying your value proposition. The next step is identifying your ideal customer and getting clear on how your startup helps them reduce a real pain point. This is a difficult point for founders who worry that they will leave someone out. But here's what happens when you focus on your ideal customer: you get more of them.

MARKETING IS NOT A ONE-SIZE-FITS-ALL

When many business owners think of marketing, they think in terms of its traditional tenets: advertising and PR. But this doesn't work for startups. By their very definition, startups are still defining product while searching for a target market. It's hard to promote something that you yourself aren't fully clear on. It's hard to track customer engagement when you're talking to everyone.

Traditional marketing also requires a significant investment that is typically out of reach when you're launching a business. Anyone who's ever considered running a TV spot during the Super Bowl understands how prohibitively expensive advertising can be, and unless you have a minimum of $100,000 a year to spend, media buys are a waste of money. As I discussed in Chapter 2, it takes, on average, seven times to become aware of an ad. It's a numbers game that only established brands can afford to play.

WORD-OF-MOUTH IS NOT MARKETING

We are all familiar with the elusive "word-of-mouth" referral, touted by founders as the Holy Grail of marketing. Once they start getting referrals, founders believe that they don't need any other type of marketing. In working with dozens of startups, I have found that the success of a "word-of-mouth" strategy is in direct proportion to the amount of work done by founders to establish their value proposition. This lays the groundwork for relevant messaging and a memorable elevator pitch that sets you apart from your competition and attracts the right customers. Too often, the elevator pitch is really a sales pitch that can quickly shut down a prospective customer. The right elevator pitch should help me quickly understand what you sell and how I can benefit from working with your company. If I'm not the right customer, all the better, since it will save you months of chasing after the wrong customer. When startups miss this critical step, messaging turns to generic content, which translates into a website that fails to convert visitors into warm leads and increase sales. Ironically, the lack of a marketing strategy reinforces a founder's confirmation bias that marketing doesn't work.

SOCIAL MEDIA IS NOT CHILD'S PLAY

For those of you who consider social media irrelevant, consider this: roughly 3.8 billion people are on social media every month, with 2.5 billion on Facebook and 1.5 billion active YouTube users. There are currently more than 500 social media sites but if you focus on your ideal customer, social media feeds become much easier to manage and scale. Instead of chasing the next social

> # 3.8 billion
>
> Active Social Media users or 49% of the world population
>
> (Kepios Analysis, 2020)

media platform "du jour," go on the sites that your customers are posting on, learn what they care about and engage with them by posting relevant content.

Get to know top bloggers and influencers in your industry and follow them on Twitter. Contribute to online conversations where you can demonstrate your expertise and build recognition as a thought leader. As you start to build followers, it adds to the perception that your startup is growing into a brand. Remember that, on average, each follower has 200+ in their network, so every new connection can turn into thousands of potential brand ambassadors.

Social media is critical in the early days of your startup. Resist the temptation to relegate this to an intern. During the first couple of years, the founder should be providing the content to make sure that they are generating the right kind of buzz for their startup. Once you have your story and key messages in place, you can hire an intern to keep your social media platforms fed on a regular basis.

> **52%**
> of online brand discovery happens in public social media feeds.
> (Hootsuite, 2020)

THE ROI OF MARKETING

Marketing is not a widget. You can't apply COGS (cost of goods sold) thinking to determine your profits. Marketing, like technology, is an investment that your company makes in its future success. Spending zero of your gross profits on marketing doesn't save you money, because your spending pie will remain the same size and you will never have money to invest in marketing. As a result, sales will be sluggish, and in five years, you'll be wondering why no one knows who you are or what you do.

Instead of waiting until you can afford traditional marketing, build a "Lean Marketing" tool box. Start with your vision—why you decided to start your business in the first place—and create relevant messaging that engages your early adopters. Instead of trying to engage with everyone, build a website that speaks to your ideal customer, and identify one or two social media channels where you can engage with them.

The longer you wait, the harder it will be to grow into a brand and establish a sustainable company culture.

It is becoming harder for brands to catch our attention as competition increases and our attention spans have decreased to 8 seconds. Each day users scroll through 300 feet of content, giving brands a very small window of time to grab the users' attention.

—**Jessica Wade**, "Social Media Marketing Trends 2018"

We'll wrap up this chapter with an exercise to help you identify your ideal client and what really matters to that client (Figure 3.1).

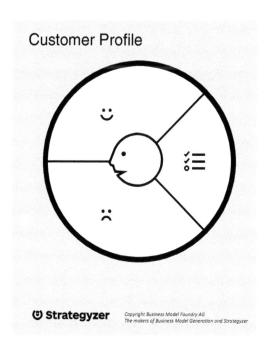

FIGURE 3.1
Customer Profile

EMPATHY MAP EXERCISE

You can use an existing customer, a composite, or an aspirational customer. Make sure to include demographics, type of industry, and job title—the more specific you are, the easier it will be to build an empathy map for them.

Make a list of customer pains and a separate list of customer gains. Identify the top three in each list. You'll want to check in with your customers to make sure you've identified the pains and gains that resonate with them. Be open to revising/refining your list.

Remember, this is about what matters to your ideal customer, not to you.

4

A Rose by Any Other Name ...

Marketing Myth #4: People buy our products in spite of our name.

> *I never felt that the naming issue was all that important, but I was obviously wrong, judging by how many people felt. I tell people to call it just plain Linux and nothing more.*
>
> —**Linus Torvalds**, creator of Linux operating system
> (originally named Freax)

A name is only as good as the story behind it. Founders can often be too close to their idea to have the perspective needed to identify the right name. And since most startups don't invest in getting clear on their brand story before they launch, they often end up choosing a name that has nothing to do with the brand they're building. As you saw in Chapter 2, even Nike had trouble scaling with the wrong name.

> *To put it simply, it's more than just a name; it's the identity of an entire brand. It deserves time and attention, and when handled properly, it'll change a business forever.*
>
> —**Adam Fridman**, founder, Mabbly, August 16, 2015

It's important to remember that the wrong name can be very costly to change. Founders often go through a naming reboot three to five years after they start the company, when it becomes clear that they've outgrown the original name. That's no surprise; it's a lot more expensive to change your name when it's on everything, from your stationery to your trade show booth, and you've invested hundreds of thousands of dollars in directing customers to your custom URL.

FOUNDER STORY: NICK BAYER, SAXBYS

Saxbys was originally founded as a coffee franchise business, but it is now a social impact company that trains college students to become successful entrepreneurs and make life better in the communities they serve.

I started Saxbys because I fell in love with the coffee industry. For me, it was never about selling coffee but about making a human connection. I wanted to make a difference in people's lives, through employment and philanthropy, and coffee was the way for me to do that.

The name: I thought a lot about the name before we opened our first café in 2005. I didn't want to name it Nick's Coffee because I didn't want it to be about me. I wanted to avoid cutesy names like "dancing goat" or "grind." I didn't want it to be about coffee because that's always been secondary to the human experience I wanted to create. Saxbys grew out of the letters from my aspirational brands—Saks Fifth Avenue, Tiffany's, Sotheby's, and Starbucks. The name was meant to be new and creative but not over the top, and one that could be easily pronounced.

The logo: The original logo was a generic coffee cup with steam coming out of it (Figure 4.1).

FIGURE 4.1
Original Saxbys Logo

By the middle of 2016, Saxbys was no longer just about building franchises but about experiential marketing and human experience and about training new entrepreneurs. The original logo didn't reflect that at all. I hired two brand consultants in Los Angeles who also represented our core customer, 18–40 female. They didn't know our brand, which made it easier for them to come to this with an open mind. They spent nine months doing focus work, studying our investors, our customers, and our marketplace. They made a series of recommendations regarding our new logo. We dropped "Coffee" from the name and replaced the generic coffee cup with a hot air balloon to reposition Saxbys from selling coffee to an uplifting hospitality experience. The fonts and new color palette energized our brand from a faded maroon to fire engine red, sky blue, and sharp black. Since I'm proud to be a Philly company, I wanted to work with a Philly designer. Regina Black, from Heads of State in Old City, crafted the final logo. Within six months, everyone had forgotten about a logo that we had for ten years. That's the power of a logo that really fits the experience it represents (Figure 4.2).

On April 13, 2017, we launched a completely new brand evolution. It was expensive but necessary. It cost roughly $200,000 to make the full change, which is why it's best not to invest in your logo the first couple of years because it will almost inevitably change. We didn't flush out "our why" in the beginning. That's why it took so long to get it right. The new logo was part of a nine-month exploration of "our why" and making sure that all touchpoints would be aligned. People forgot our old logo because the new one is completely aligned with who we are.

FIGURE 4.2
Current Saxbys Logo

The original concept was to build a chain of franchises, and I foolishly tried to franchise right out of the gate. To build a successful franchise, you first have to run a business for a few years so you understand what you're doing. From the start, we were focused on selling franchises. I wanted to grow rapidly and all at once. That was a mistake. Marketing for me was a great website, being on brand, being visionary, and opening our first café in downtown Atlanta. At the start of my business, marketing was focused on driving customers to the café; instead, it should have been focused on driving product. I was an early adopter of experiential marketing. I wanted people to experience the brand, get excited about the concept, and say: "I want to bring this to my hometown." The website worked, but it was based on the wrong thing. Having people experience the brand worked really well. In fact, it worked better than it should have. We had hundreds, if not thousands of requests for franchises. We gave franchise tours and thousands of people came in. I wished I'd had a better product. We focused on the front end—the sizzle—and less on the steak side. We used the website to sell franchises. We should have used it to sell $4 lattes and $5 smoothies.

> *I realized that we needed to change the heart of our brand, so we gave ourselves a heart transplant.*
>
> —**Nick Bayer**, founder and CEO, Saxbys

I've always been against what people would call soft openings. We generate all our revenue through a cash business, so I've always felt that the day you open, you need to create tremendous excitement for your business. This turned out to be a mistake that didn't serve us well.

The day we opened Saxbys at 1800 Chestnut in Center City, Philadelphia, customers could pay as they wished and Saxbys matched dollar for dollar to our scholarship fund. We had the mayor, Eagles players, and politicians acting as celebrity baristas. It was wall-to-wall for nine straight hours. Customers couldn't get in and the new team members were completely overwhelmed. But as a result, we created tremendous external buzz. The next day, the store was much quieter, and our inventory was blown out. Team members didn't get to have a normal day so there was this whole domino effect—they couldn't relate well to how the business would operate on a regular day. So, when we opened 1818 Market Street, we did the opposite. During our training, we explained what opening day would be like so the team would be ready. We waited a month before the official opening.

That gave the team time to work together and get used to running the store. When we had the grand opening with celebrity baristas, it gave the new café a jolt in the arm. But this time, we knew what we were doing and we were ready for the jolt. This became our new model, and we've opened every new store the same way since.

Advice to Founders

Get your "why" down. Why are consumers going to care about your brand? You need to have the discipline to communicate it really well across all touchpoints, not just the obvious stuff like your website. Your employees need to be committed to your brand and be willing to advocate for it. During our catch-up period, we grew dramatically when we figured out our why.

I was in business for five years before I considered the question of who we were as a brand. And when I asked the question, I realized that we needed to change the heart of our brand, so we gave ourselves a heart transplant. We now know who we are and why we exist. We provide an experience and work with each of the campus communities where we have a coffee shop to improve the community. We give money back to education through scholarships at Community College of Philadelphia. We educate future entrepreneurs by taking classroom learning and making it real in a business setting and teaching them the skills they need to succeed. Each coffee shop is a student franchise run exclusively by students. Each coffee shop is supported through our franchise model but runs as a standalone brand.

We now use our headquarters to help people "get" our brand, to "drink the Kool-Aid." We want potential hires and investors to see what is going on here and why our people love what we do. I often hear that we must have the best training there is, but I know that it's more of a testament to how we recruit than how we train. If a potential hire is not a culture fit, you can have the best training in the world, but the output will still be wrong.

Epilogue

Today, Saxbys has 25 coffee shops, 616 employees, and roughly $15 million in annual revenues. Saxbys has more than 18,000 followers on Facebook, 16,000 on Instagram, nearly 6,000 on Twitter, and more than 7,000 on LinkedIn. Their current website highlights their social mission, helps you find your local Saxbys, and offers catering and products for sale. The Saxbys Fellows Endowed Fund at Temple University offers a $60,000 fund to help students achieve and exceed academic goals.

BE MEMORABLE

Brand is the sum of all experiences that your customers have with your company. It happens over time and on multiple channels and lives in the minds of your customers. In his book *Building Strong Brands,* David Aaker explains that great brands live in our minds, on a virtual shelf of our own making. There is only room for four or five brands on that shelf, and once a brand has been placed there, it's nearly impossible for it to fall off the shelf. That's why brands like Nike spend so much money; to ensure that their brand never falls off that shelf.

Branding refers to the identity of your brand and includes your name, logo, colors, and even the shape of your products. Think of it as the face of your business.

Adam Fridman, founder of the digital marketing agency Mabbly, notes that your company name is "more than just a name; it's the identity of an entire brand. It deserves time and attention, and when handled properly, it'll change a business forever."[1]

Branding is critical to word-of-mouth referrals. But it works only if your brand delivers a memorable experience that your customers are excited to share.

The first thing a customer interacts with is a name, so it has to convey the right message; it has to wow the audience. Think of it as a first handshake; it says a lot about the person and makes a powerful impression.

—**Adam Fridman**, founder, Mabbly

LOGO IS SHORTHAND FOR YOUR BRAND

When we see that iconic swoosh, we recognize Nike and instantly images of athletes in Nike gear pop up in our minds. When we catch a glimpse of golden arches, we recognize McDonald's. Don't rush to get a logo until you're sure you have the name that will grow with your company and are clear on what that logo should represent. A good logo sums up a customer's entire experience with the brand.

The founders of AI-powered logo design and branding platform, Taylor Brands, note that "logos are a point of identification; they're the symbol that customers use to recognize your brand. Ideally, you'll want people to instantly connect the sight of your logo with the memory of what your company does – and, more importantly, how it makes them feel."[2]

BRAND LOYALTY STARTS WITH THE RIGHT NAME

In his book *The Brand Gap*, Marty Neumeier tells us that the need for good brand names is driven by customers who "will always want convenient ways of identifying, remembering, discussing, and comparing brands." Neumeier makes the case that the right name is a valuable asset that drives differentiation and speeds up the process of integrating a new brand into our collective consciousness. Most importantly, the wrong name can cost millions, even billions, over the lifetime of the brand.

> *George Bernard Shaw's advice applies to brands as well as people: "Take care to get born well."*
>
> —**Marty Neumeier**, author

Names are also important to a family's identity and can have long-lasting effects. A colleague's family was originally known as Ruzzo—a common name in Sicily where their peasant ancestors came from. In 1901, when my colleague's great-grandfather came through Ellis Island, he was "renamed" Russo because to the untrained ear of the immigration officials, the Italian pronunciation of Ruzzo sounded a lot like Russo but with a very different meaning. The name Russo, or "Red" in Italian, comes from the Latin *rubius* and *rossius* and is associated with royalty, with its own family crest that features a red lion on its hind legs.

What strikes me about this story is how quintessentially American it is. What immigrant doesn't dream of discarding their old life for a new and better one in their adopted country? America was founded on such stories of reinvention.

My family originally came from Romania, and my father grew up with the common last name of Lupu, which means "Wolf" in Romanian, from the Latin, *lupus*. When my father immigrated to Israel after World War II, he changed his name to Zevi, which means "Wolf" in Hebrew. When my family immigrated to the United States in the late 1960s, people had a hard time pronouncing our last name, so it became "Americanized." Zevi became Zeewy, and the name stuck. In the process, I lost a piece of my family's history, and my name became a conversation starter and a mystery to be solved.

It turns out that names are as important to a company's identity as they are to an individual. When done well, a company's name (together with a memorable logo and tagline) becomes the face of that business. The right name helps potential customers remember you, which is the first step to growing sales and revenue. Successful companies recognize the power of a good name and the limitations of a generic one—and they change the name when they are ready for growth. During a merger or acquisition, the name with the greatest recognition wins the identity battle.

It bears repeating that Nike, the recognized leader in athletic wear, was known as Blue Ribbon Sports until 1971, when they launched their first iconic running shoe, the Nike Waffle Trainer. It's hard to imagine Blue Ribbon Sports endorsed by basketball legend Michael Jordan or growing into the brand of choice worn by Olympic athletes worldwide. It's much too small a name for such a global brand.

GREAT NAMES: GREAT BRANDS

Ever wonder how some of your favorite brands got their names?

Google comes from "googol" representing the number 1 followed by 100 zeros, and it's the perfect name for a search engine company. The name was added to Webster's dictionary in 2007 and is now used as both a noun and a verb. Not surprisingly, I googled the name to learn its meaning.

IKEA is a random collection of letters that represent the founder's name and the Swedish property and village where he grew up: Ingvar Kamprad Elmtaryd Agunnaryd. His Swedish identity is imbedded in the store's DNA and even in the food they serve in the cafeteria.

LEGO is a combination of the Danish phrase "leg godt," which translates to "play well." Coincidentally, Lego also means "I put together" in Latin.

My immigration story sparked a search for my own identity and a life-long fascination with names. It also led me to a lifelong career helping others uncover and live their authentic identity. Isn't that what America is all about?

We'll wrap up this chapter with an exercise to help you develop the right name for your startup.

NAMING EXERCISE

According to Marketing MO,[3] the most common types of names:

- Use the founder or inventor's name (Ford)
- Describe what you do (British Airways)
- Describe an experience or image (Wizz Air)
- Take a word out of context (Apple)
- Make up a word (Etsy)

1. List as many words/two- or three-word sentences (50–100) that come to mind when you think of your startup. For inspiration, look at names from Greek mythology and foreign translations of your favorite words.
2. Organize the words/sentences into buckets.
3. Come up with three names based on words from the bucket with the most words.
4. Take your three names on a test run and see which one resonates with friends, colleagues, and trusted advisors.
5. Wait a while before you build a website around your new name. Remember, you'll be living with this name for a long time, so don't rush to put something out there before you've vetted it.

Once you have a name, do a first-page Google search and then contact an intellectual property (IP) attorney to rule out any potential infringement issues. If your chosen name is free and clear, copyright it and secure your website address (URL).

NOTES

1 https://www.inc.com/adam-fridman/why-your-company-name-is-as-important-as-your-company-function-adam.html.
2 https://www.tailorbrands.com/logo-maker/why-a-logo-is-important
3 http://www.marketingmo.com/creative-brand-development/how-to-choose-a-great-brand-name

5

Is Your Homepage Helping Your Brand Cut Through the Noise?

Marketing Myth #5: Customers expect a website, but it's not critical to our business.

> *Great web design without functionality is like a sports car without an engine.*
>
> —**Paul Cookson**, poet

Your website is your brand's house, and your homepage its front door. Yet, many a startup's website lacks a user-centered framework. The content is typically all about what the company does and how well they do it. It's internally focused instead of appealing to what customers care about. The goal of your homepage is to answer two critical questions in the mind of the user: Why am I here, and why should I care? Users make a go/no-go decision in roughly six seconds, so if you don't help them connect with your brand quickly, they leave and don't come back. More importantly, they don't tell anyone about you. As a result, sales don't come through the website, and this reinforces the paradigm that a website is not critical to sales or marketing.

According to computer researcher Daniel S. Fowler, there are roughly 1.7 billion websites in the world. Yet, most get no visitors.

FOUNDER STORY: NANCY MACINTYRE, FINGERPRINT

Fingerprint is a mobile app for children

My company came out of K2 Media Labs, a business incubator in New York, and its founders Daniel Klaus and Kevin Wendel became my cofounders. They served as my advisors and still sit on my board. We launched Fingerprint (fingerprintplay.com) in 2011. From the start, we realized that we needed to be clear on who we were talking to and what would be appropriate for them to know. I hired a PR firm within the first year to help me get clear on how to talk to each of our audiences. We continually invested in making everything related to our brand bigger, more professional, and more deliberate than our competitors. Before I founded this startup, I was Executive Vice President at Leapfrog Enterprises, and prior to that I was Vice President of Sales and Marketing at Lucas Arts, a division of Lucas Films. Because of my marketing background, I knew how to talk to customers, the press, and media outlets, and how to use marketing effectively. PR works best when you're able to say to your agency, here's our positioning, and then hand over 90% of the work. Anyone starting a company should be an expert in marketing, or they shouldn't do it. If I had been a Chief Technology Officer (CTO) with no idea how to sell a new product in the market, it would have cost a lot more to build out our marketing. Understanding who we were was invaluable to the success of our startup.

> *From the start, I realized that we needed to be clear on who we were talking to and what would be appropriate for them to know.*
>
> —**Nancy MacIntyre**, founder, Fingerprint

From the start, we invested in mobile advertising to drive downloads of our products. This worked really well in driving downloads. We identified three or four metrics we were going to need to focus on in our marketing and started driving those vanity metrics—messaging that would be exciting to consumers and partners. Our goal was to get to 100,000 downloads. We put in a tracker like the one used in Times Square, to track the number of minutes that people played with our app. In one month, we had more than 100,000 downloads and one million users.

That gave us metrics to use in press releases and post on our social media feeds. For example, we could point to the fact that kids from thirty-seven states were playing our app. That became a soundbite to get people to write about us. Scalability was built around the simple idea of establishing vanity metrics to use in all our communications, tracking them and using them everywhere. Instead of relying on others to write our narrative, we drove the conversations. We put the millions of minutes of play in perspective, so that people could relate to those numbers in a meaningful way. In January, we had tracked 14.9 million sessions with an average of thirty-two minutes per session.

We put a lot of energy into getting bloggers to write about us. We found that influential "mommy bloggers" and app developers were key to growing social media followers. We sent online press packets to hundreds of bloggers, and to lead reviewers in *USA Today*, the *New York Times*, and other influential publications. We were successful in getting people to cover us, but it didn't increase our customer base, and leading app reviews didn't move the needle at all. We had a PR person spending all of her time to get coverage, but it didn't drive downloads. It was a waste of time and money. If I were launching my startup today, I would do less. At the time, I tried to do way too much. Instead of launching one app and moving on to the second, third, and fourth apps, we launched all of them at once. No one would review all four apps, so we had to choose which child to put our marketing money on.

Investors know that building product and infrastructure is a small aspect of launching an app. You need to think about how you're going to get your app discovered in stores and how you'll get consumers to find it. Every business is different. If you're starting an online restaurant, you'll have to buy consumers. How you spend your marketing dollars should be based on your objectives. The goal is to attract investors who are willing to invest in your startup. We spent $50,000 on PR to get someone to read an article about us in the *New York Times*, which led to a $5M investment.

As founders we have to have the discipline to ask the right questions. The question is not how much can I afford, but what am I trying to do? Then, how much will it cost and can I afford it? Without money, how do I create interesting assets for free?

As a startup you don't have money for traditional marketing. Founders have to get super comfortable with social media, to build a Twitter base for themselves, their co-founders, and their company. You have to build up your customer base on Facebook, LinkedIn, Instagram, to put it all out there. You also have to blend personal with professional and bring everyone you know into this journey with you. Whatever category you're in, get in groups and associate with folks with shared interests, and build that network. Every business should be building an email database. It costs you nothing to build and is the cheapest way to market your startup. There is nothing more important for a founder than to bring in customers and raise money. If you don't bring in customers, you have no money. It's that simple. It's fine to bring in an intern to manage your social media feeds, but it's critical to your startup's success for the founder to put themselves out there and engage with strategic partners and editors, and to be true and authentic.

> *The question is not how much can I afford, but what am I trying to do? … [H]ow much will it cost and can I afford to do it?*
>
> —**Nancy MacIntyre**, founder, Fingerprint

Digital marketing investment is different from traditional investment. As a founder, you have to think in terms of customer acquisition and what the lifetime value of your customer will be. A good rule to follow is to spend less than one-third of the lifetime value of a customer. You need to think of customer acquisition as a sales funnel with a layered approach; first you have to get them to like your Facebook page; then to download their email address, so you can send them an email to start the trial; then let them use your app for a while, before you can convert them to a paying customer. Ultimately, you'll need to decide for yourself how much you can afford to spend per customer. In digital marketing, the advertising-to-sales ratio is 8% so you can afford to spend $4.00 per product for marketing.

With a subscription model like ours, you're investing heavily in the customer upfront and the payback comes back over the lifetime of that customer. You may need to invest $30 to get someone to play for free, to keep playing, and eventually to buy your app and keep buying other apps.

The idea of following businesses is really old school. If you're creating a relevant stream of social media content, customers will find you and follow you. That's why it's critical to identify the topics that people care about, so they will follow you. Growth will happen organically. Programming a news show or newsletter in real time, posting every day, and hoping people are sharing it, that's content marketing, and it's what we do every day.

The website is often the best place to get product information because customers can do a deep dive there. They can watch videos, download an article, or read your press coverage. Your marketing has to be omni-channeled to attract customers—From Facebook, to Instagram, to e-commerce, to your website. Each has a role in engaging with consumers. It's all about pushing out content. As a founder, my job was to drive one overarching strategy and then task different people with the job of creating content and putting it out on social media.

We wanted to get coverage for a new game that *Highlights* launched that would drive it to the number one game during Super Bowl Sunday 2016. I had no idea how much it would cost, so I convinced *Highlights* to write an advance press release and run it. That press release drove our app up to the number one iPad game. It was a simple but effective way to drive the conversation. *Highlights* was the #1 app on Super Bowl Sunday 2016. It was our biggest day ever, and we got a ton of free publicity. Other people wrote articles about it. We couldn't have manufactured this kind of press. We released the app the day before the Super Bowl. This is a great example of what you can do without a lot of money.

Advice to Founders

I think the biggest success factor in marketing your startup is to understand what it is, how it's positioned, and get crystal clear on messaging, and then develop a marketing plan that spells out how it will achieve your marketing goal. A lot of people operate under the philosophy of "if you build it, they will come" or treat it like a widget where you spend a dollar and expect a return based on your balance sheet. If I had been more rigorous in the beginning, I would have gotten really clear on what I wanted to do, spent money towards that goal, and iterate only when I understood how all of the pieces went together. You can't tell the consumer what to think, and you can't get consumers to buy a product based on an ad. Consumers will go on Yelp and if they read a review on the company's bad customer service or if they don't like your pricing structure, they will write about it. Consumers don't get an impression of your brand from you, but from your customers. What you say, how you say it, and how you keep long-term relationships—that's what consumers will pay attention to. Marketing won't help you if your customers don't like your product.

Epilogue

Today Fingerprint has nearly 50,000 followers on Facebook, close to 9,000 followers on Twitter, and more than 2,000 monthly viewers on Pinterest.

YOUR WEBSITE IS A CRITICAL MARKETING TOOL

Getting a quality website is not an expense but rather an investment.

—**Dr. Christopher Dayagdag**, CEO, Marketing Link Web Solutions

It's hard to remember a time when the World Wide Web was not a fixture in our lives, and even harder to believe that when it became publicly available on August 6, 1991, there was no fanfare in the global press or mass consumer frenzy. For most of us, it was just another Tuesday. Its creator, Tim Berners-Lee, posted what amounted to an academic white paper on the alt.hypertext newsgroup,[1] and with it, gave birth to a new technology that would fundamentally change the world as we knew it.

In those early Wild West days, a website was a glorified brochure with contact information. The idea of having 24/7 access was so novel that just being able to read about a company from the comfort of your own computer was enough to generate sales and build a customer base. Once people realized that they were no longer limited by place or time, business communication radically changed and the number of daily emails exploded. The Internet didn't create emails but it did put them on a super highway. The first email message was sent on October 29, 1969 from computer to computer on ARPANET (Advanced Research Projects Agency Network) as shown in Figure 5.1.[2]

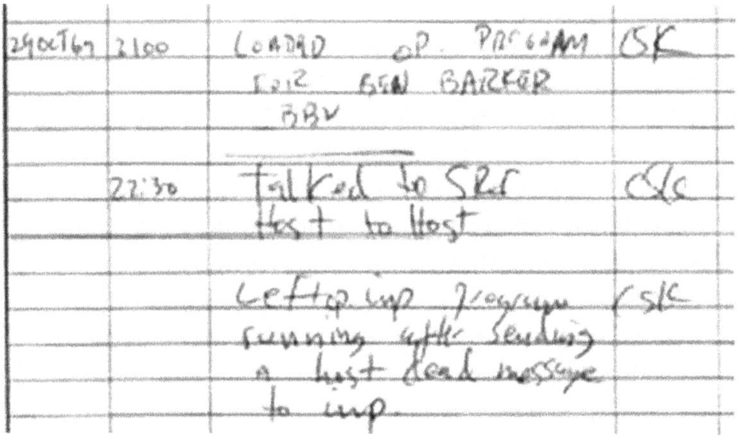

FIGURE 5.1
The First Email

In "A Brief History of Email: Dedicated to Ray Tomlinson," the UK marketing firm Phrasee notes that "although email can be found on computers at MIT in a program called 'MAILBOX' all the way back in 1965," it was Ray Tomlinson who in 1971, "invented and developed electronic mail as we know it today by creating ARPANET's networked email system."[3] The first text message was sent on December 3, 1992,[4] nearly ten years before cell phones were introduced to consumers.

Since its inception, email has evolved into the most popular form of communication in the world. In 2019, more than half the world population used email and the number of business and consumer emails that were sent and received was more than 293 billion.[5]

As technology advances at ever-increasing rates, so have consumer buying habits—and with them, the way they interact with their brands. Today, websites are expected to provide an exceptional user experience, one that consumers can share and engage in with thousands, in a virtual community of like-minded brand enthusiasts. These days, a basic site no longer helps a company stand out. It feels as innovative as a rotary phone.

CUTTING THROUGH THE NOISE

As noted earlier, there are roughly 1.7 billion websites in the world with an average of 500,000 launched every day. Most websites get no traffic at all. Roughly 10 million sites (0.01%) get more than 50% of all visitors. Think Google, YouTube, and Facebook. I've seen hundreds of websites in nearly twenty years of working with startups, and I often hear from founders that their web-site doesn't matter all that much since no business comes from it. What they are really saying is that they are still thinking of their website as a digital brochure. Consequently, their content is falling on deaf ears. Often, they don't consider the importance of speed and how quickly their website uploads on mobile devices. Brochures were physical experiences meant to be read over time. Websites have taken our business communication on a superhighway, and it's hard to compete if you're riding a bicycle.

> **$500 million**
> amount of money lost each year due to slow websites (WebsiteHostingRating.com 2020)

As I've already mentioned, the typical company website is created with little regard for the end user's needs and interests. Instead, they're all about themselves. But the fact is, customers don't care about you. They care about what happens when they work with you and/or use your product. They care about the results that only you can deliver. It's also good to remember that as technology has sped up, so have the ever-increasing stimuli competing for our attention. Breaking through the noise is not just a catchphrase, but a business imperative.

YOUR BRAND'S FRONT DOOR

If your website is your brand's house and your homepage its front door, then your domain is your brand's address. Most of us would never put the entire contents of our bedroom closet, our living room furniture, and kitchen appliances outside our front door. Yet, that's exactly what many company homepages do. Executives worry that a critical piece of information will get left out and, as a result, they load up their homepages with lots of internal-focused content, from the latest hire to the company's history.

The onus is on the web visitors to figure out how to navigate the content provided and whether or not it's relevant to them. Since most people make a go/no-go decision in seconds, busy homepages typically shut down any desire to click further and greatly reduce the odds that a visitor will become a prospect. Then, when conversion rates fall flat and sales don't come through the website, it reinforces the founder's confirmation bias that a website isn't critical to the growth of their business. The average CEO has 930 LinkedIn connections, so you've lost not only a potential customer, but a brand advocate who could promote you to their network.

930

LinkedIn connections of the average CEO.

(Omnicore Blogpost, 2020)

The revenue impact from a 10%-point improvement in a company's customer experience score can translate into more than $1B.

—**Joe Rinaldi**, "30 Eye-Opening User Experience Stats"

Your website should make it easy for consumers to research your products and/or services and do a deep dive into your company. It should provide a navigation system that makes it easy to watch videos, listen to a podcast, read your blog posts, and connect to your social media feeds. Your home page is a critical entry point in a multi-channel content strategy that includes social media feeds

79%

of people who don't like what they find on one site will search for another site.

(Impact Learning Center, 2017)

like Facebook, Twitter, and Instagram so you can engage your customers. Your website should push out content that your customers care about and help nurture relationships that will eventually turn into a vocal and passionate community of brand evangelists.

If you build *that,* they will come.

We'll wrap up this chapter with a messaging exercise to help you engage and retain your ideal customer.

MESSAGING EXERCISE

Complete this sentence:

When I talk to a potential customer about my business, I always mention that …

Write a sentence that sums up what you've identified as your brand promise. It should be specific and action-oriented. Use the present tense and avoid words ending in -ing and passive verbs like "help." You are putting a stake in the ground and saying, this is who we are and what we do for our customers.

Go back to the empathy exercise at the end of Chapter 3 and identify the top three things that matter to your ideal customer. You can choose from the pains and/or gains column. The point of this exercise is to become clear on how you solve a real pain point and/or provide a real gain to your ideal customer.

Now write three sentences that describe what your ideal customer gets from working with you and only you. This should include how your brand solves a problem that truly matters to that customer. Each sentence should focus on one key message.

NOTES

1 https://timeline.web.cern.ch/sir-berners-lee-announces-www-software-internet
2 https://phrasee.co/a-brief-history-of-email/
3 https://phrasee.co/a-brief-history-of-email/
4 https://www.npr.org/2017/12/04/568393428/the-first-text-messages-celebrates-25-years
5 https://www.lifewire.com/how-many-emails-are-sent-every-day-1171210

6

The New Age of Commerce

Marketing Myth #6: Social media is for Millennials.

> *We don't have a choice whether we do social media.
> The question is how well we do it.*

—**Erik Qualman**, author, *What Happens in Vegas Stays on YouTube*

There are hundreds of social media platforms, but most startups only need to focus on Facebook, Instagram, Twitter, and LinkedIn. That's because in the first year the goal is to build credibility and brand awareness. Also, because 80% of Pinterest users are women, unless your product or service is aimed exclusively at women, it's not the right platform for you. Here is the breakdown of social media use by U.S. adults:[1]

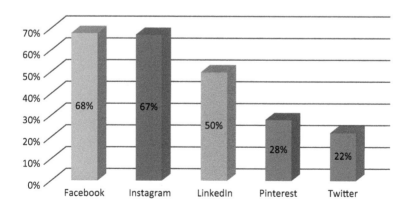

Founders often get overwhelmed by the volume of social media and wrongly assume that because they can't navigate it, their customers can't either. This is why many founders I spoke with handed over the responsibility for social media to a young intern. But that's not a strategy. It's a default position that always leads to the same result: social media feeds that fail to engage the right customers with the right message. You can't build a rabid fan base if your content is out of synch with your customers.

FOUNDER STORY: BRYNNE TILLMAN, SOCIAL SALES LINK

Social Sales Link teaches corporate teams and entrepreneurs how to leverage the power of LinkedIn for social selling.

I've been in sales training my whole career. Prior to launching Social Sales Link in 2013, I was a partner in a sales training company. I taught LinkedIn as a loss leader to bring people into our training program and I learned that I was not a phenomenal sales trainer. My little sliver of genius turned out to be leveraging LinkedIn for sales. When I left to start my company, I was able to grow quickly by providing weekly content and following up with people who engaged with my content. I wrote weekly blogs and offered simple PDF downloads with information and tips to help people grow their sales and increase revenue through their LinkedIn connections. I created polls and short videos and captured quotes from people who responded to my polls on a variety of topics. I turned quotes into one-line posts and added graphics because images increase click rates. I wrote e-books using those quotes and recognized the people who contributed to my weekly posts.

> *"It's not about you. It's about them. Don't lead with your solutions. Lead people to your solutions."*
>
> —**Brynne Tillman**, founder and CEO, Social Sales Link

My first e-book was *The LinkedIn Sales Playbook*. It got roughly 800,000 views. I wrote and published a simple checklist with ten tips from my book. I offered it to my LinkedIn network as a free PDF download. That checklist got more than 15,000 downloads and went viral—before hashtags. It was not sophisticated, but people remembered me. I learned that the key to engagement is to focus on what people need to succeed. I didn't talk about sales training. There was no call to action. I mined each of my contacts to find people in their network who could be potential customers and posted a weekly blog with a link to each blogpost. I built a 26,000-member mailing list through those posts. I applied the same social selling principles we teach our clients to use.

Listen to your customers, offer them useful content on a regular basis, and engage with them. It's not about you. It's about them. Don't lead with your solutions. Lead people to your solutions.

When you're a solopreneur, you are the brand. I built my brand on my name and people recognize and trust the Brynne Tillman name. We now have a seven-person team and are looking to add two more people this year. We have to figure out how to transition from the Brynne Tillman Brand to the Social Sales Link Brand.

In 2020, Social Sales Link launched a program for coaches and entrepreneurs. We offer free webinars, a content library for e-learning, and monthly group coaching. We've built an online community where people can learn from each other as well as from our coaches. We purposely made it affordable so we can help as many business owners as possible. As an entrepreneur, you have to earn the right to a sale before someone will buy from you. One member of our coaching group earned $3 million through our process.

Advice to Founders

I should have outsourced as much as possible so I could focus on what I do best—bringing in new clients and serving those clients. I made the mistake of separating sales from marketing. I'm a great sales person so I thought that I didn't need marketing. I only focused on outbound sales from people who already knew me through my LinkedIn network. The problem is that you have to keep selling again and again. Marketing would have brought in a steady stream of inbound traffic from people who didn't know me or my company. If I had invested in marketing from the beginning, I would have been able to establish a recurring revenue model and scale faster. Instead of building my own WordPress site, I should have hired a web professional or partnered with a fractional Chief Marketing Officer to build a professional website and help us maximize our user experience. We optimized SEO to drive lots of traffic to our website, but our conversion rate is still very low. There's nothing compelling visitors to move through our website and join our ecosystem. I didn't understand the user journey from a client's perspective and that's hurt us.

"I'm a great sales person so when I started my business, I thought that I didn't need marketing. The problem is that I have to sell again and again. If I had invested in marketing from the beginning, I would have been able to establish a recurring revenue model and scale faster."
—**Brynne Tillman**, founder and CEO, Social Sales Link

Michael E. Gerber, the author of *The E-Myth* advises founders to build out their process so that if they went away for a month and had to hand their company to anyone in their company, they could do it. We finally documented all of our processes because it's really hard to scale your business if you're the only one who knows how everything works.

Epilogue

Social Sales Link has created and led corporate training programs for more than 30 banks and leading corporations such as Penn Mutual, McKesson, and Aramark. As of 2020, more than 100,000 people have gone through the Social Sales Link training program. Brynne Tillman has 22,000 followers on Twitter and more than 60,000 people follow her LinkedIn posts. She has maxed out at 30,000 LinkedIn connections, the highest number allowed on the platform.

WELCOME TO THE NEW AGE OF COMMERCE

Think of all the ways everyday life has changed as a result of technology. Once upon a time—think 1985—the only way to purchase a product was to go to a brick-and-mortar location, also known as a store, to check it out before making a purchase. It was highly transactional and limited to how much time a customer was willing to spend on comparison shopping. It took a lot of time and energy, and the power was heavily weighted in favor of the seller.

To remain relevant, businesses must shift from transactional thinking to relationship building, or go out of business.

Despite the profound influence of technology on our lives, companies are still trying to figure out how to influence customer habits and their purchasing decisions. Armed with smartphones, customers now take their commerce with them and do price comparisons on the go, without the need to ever see a product in "real time." To remain relevant, businesses must shift from transactional thinking to relationship building, or go out of business.

As of February 2020, there were nearly 7.8 billion people on the planet. More than half (roughly 4 billion) are on the Internet, and more than 75% of those are active social media users. Nearly all active social media users are on smartphones.

> **3.8 billion**
> people or 50% of the world's population uses social media.
> (Hootsuite, The Global State of Digital, 2020)

There are currently more than 500 social media sites, but social media becomes much easier to manage and scale if you think about your ideal customer. Instead of chasing the next social media platform *du jour*, go on the sites that your customers are posting on, learn what they care about, and engage them with relevant content.

THINK LIKE A MILLENNIAL

Millennials (people born between 1982 and 2004) have forever changed how we do business. At 70 million, they represent the largest population in the United States. By 2025, they will make up 75% of the workforce. More than 85% of Millennials own a smartphone and use it for everything from calling an Uber to downloading their resume. To put this in perspective, in five years, three quarters of the world's population will do all their business using mobile technology, and the decisions they make will be based largely on their interactions on social media. This global shift will impact everything and everyone.

> **75%**
> of Instagram users follow calls to action.
> (Thump Creative, 2020)

Unlike GenXers before them, Millennials are immune to traditional branded content and instead turn to their social media network for recommendations before making a buying decision. They don't watch TV, and they don't read newspapers. They go on Instagram and Facebook to connect with their favorite brands and stay ahead of emerging trends. They follow influencers and thought leaders on Twitter and go to LinkedIn to research companies and learn more about company leaders. If you're selling a consumer product and you don't have a social media strategy, you run the risk of becoming invisible.

DON'T SELL ME; HELP ME DISCOVER

In ancient times, otherwise known as the 20th century, companies acquired customers through a workforce well-versed in established sales practices, a compelling pitch, and the personality of their salespeople. The Digital Revolution has changed not only how customers buy, but how companies acquire customers.

Millennials don't want to be sold; they want to discover your company through relevant content and meaningful engagement. They pay attention to a company's core values to see if they align with theirs and look for ways to connect with brands. This is why social media is so powerful. It provides infinite opportunities for engagement and allows companies to see what content connects with potential customers and get feedback in real time. Patagonia has more than 400,000 followers on Twitter who support their sustainable practices and their mission to do no harm and help protect the planet. Their customers are extreme sports enthusiasts who proudly wear Patagonia to explore the world while they promote their brand's products. Donna Karan has been a leading fashion brand since 1984 and has remained relevant in a highly competitive industry through social media. Their one million-plus Facebook followers stay connected because they know that DKNY offers them the latest New York lifestyle news as well as product updates (Figure 6.1).

To get the most out of social media for your brand, start by identifying your ideal customer and what matters to them. Once you know who they are, do your research, find out which social media platforms they spend time on, and go there. Look at who and what they engage with so you can create relevant content that will get shared with people in their network and help you reach new customers.

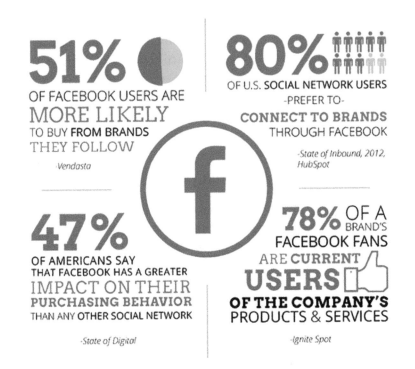

FIGURE 6.1
Facebook Statistics

If you post something and hear crickets, reboot and try again. Content on Facebook has a shelf life of five hours. The posts don't go away, but their efficacy wanes, and your customers are less likely to engage with them after that time. Contrast this with blogs which have a two-year shelf life. This is good news if you're a blogger, because it gives you a chance to build an audience over a longer period of time. For authors, blogs are a great way to parcel out sections of content to use on their social media feeds that can get them in front of potential readers and publishers (Figure 6.2).

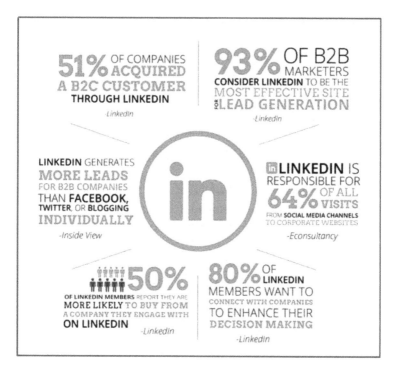

FIGURE 6.2
LinkedIn Statistics

LinkedIn is used primarily for business development and to find talent, which is why 90% of recruiters use LinkedIn to find job candidates. A LinkedIn post gets the most traffic for the first twenty-four hours which is the amount of time that recruiters expect to get responses to a job posting. Facebook is the perfect platform for checking out your competition and for measuring your company against theirs. If you're looking for a job, Facebook provides a window into a company's culture. Twitter is a powerful tool for trying out a new idea or concept and adding your thoughts to an influencer's. It's also a great way for a startup to build followers and see if there's a potential customer for their new idea.

We'll wrap up this chapter with an exercise to help you pick the right social media platform for your new company.

―――――

SOCIAL MEDIA EXERCISE

Circle the description(s) that best fit what you do or want to achieve:

1. I sell a product/service that helps my clients promote their local events, and my goal is to help build a community.
2. I want to establish myself and my startup as a thought leader in my industry.
3. I want to connect with influencers.
4. I am in the creative industry and use a lot of visuals to tell my brand story.
5. I am building a web-based business with how-to tutorials and free content to help educate and attract my ideal customer.

If you circled #1, you'll want to be on Facebook.
If you circled #2, you'll want to be on LinkedIn.
If you circled #3, you'll want to be on Twitter.
If you circled #4, you'll want to be on Instagram.
If you circled #5, you'll want to build a YouTube following.

―――――

NOTE

1 https://www.oberlo.com/blog/social-media-marketing-statistics

7

Is Your Story Button On?

Marketing Myth #7: Great products sell themselves.

*Marketing and branding are some of the
most important early-stage indicators of a
company's potential success.*

—**Mamoon Hamid**, "Debunking the 7 Myths of Marketing in the Enterprise"

A great product is important, but great product marketing is critical. You have to continually sell your brand's value proposition and showcase your product as the hero in your customer's journey. Engagement is key. Social media channels help bring your story home by showing your product in use and building a compelling narrative.

Customers need to be able to say—instinctively and immediately—"I get what this does for me. I understand how to adopt and deploy it, and it helps me do what I need to get done faster and better." Even if you're a two-person company, you can make yourself look open for business and make it seem much bigger than you actually are. It can be a self-fulfilling prophecy, as success begets success.

FOUNDER STORY: JOE BORN, COO, IMAGIROO, LLC

Imagiroo grew out of the Kangaroo Cup, a product created by 11-year-old Lily Born. In 2014, 13-year-old Lily was recognized as a CNN Hero.

Lily Born was only eight years old when she noticed that her grandfather, who has Parkinson's disease, kept knocking over his cup. So, she came up with the idea for a three-legged cup that wouldn't tip over—and the Kangaroo Cup was born. Like every good industrial designer, she spent several years prototyping, first with hand-moldable plastic and then with clay. Her father, Joe Born, encouraged her to take her idea into production and helped her get it produced. The Kangaroo Cup took five years to evolve from a sketch into a consumer product that is now manufactured in China and in Southern California.

> *In 2012, The Kangaroo Cup Indiegogo crowdfunding campaign raised $12,877. In 2014, our Kickstarter campaign raised $62,053. In total, more than 10,000 cups were sold.*
>
> —**Joe Born**, COO, Imagiroo

Marketing has dominated this product since the first Kickstarter campaign in 2012. The Kangaroo Cup went through two crowdfunding campaigns. The first Indiegogo campaign was in the fall of 2012 and sold 1,000 cups. We were in China when we launched a Kickstarter campaign in the spring of 2014 and Lily's story went viral. Lilly Dunn, a design blogger at Fast Company, contacted me to ask if she could interview Lily for the magazine and in the fall of that year, the *Chicago Tribune* picked up her story.

The press loved Lily's story. She was invited to the White House Science Fair and got the chance to tour the China Room in the White House. The Science Fair didn't help us sell our product, but it added visibility to Lily's story and gave the Kangaroo Cup credibility. Then *The Tonight Show* called and Lily was nominated as a CNN Hero. Although the invitation to come on *The Tonight Show* fell through, the publicity

2

around her story helped launch our second Kickstarter campaign. The red-carpet, CNN Heroes event made Lily famous. She had just turned 13, and she was treated like a celebrity.

Our second Kickstarter campaign sold more than 10,000 Kangaroo Cups, but we didn't have the staff to help push the product out. Instead, we waited for the groundswell to get bigger and talked to distributors about Lily's story. Because of our size, we weren't able to partner with well-known brands like OXO, which would have been a game-changer for us. It's one thing to have a great story, but it's quite another to scale production and sell a product to millions of customers.

Good storytelling builds brand awareness.
—**Joe Born**, COO, Imagiroo

Storytelling matters and is central to sales. Telling a genuine story helps distinguish a product like this from other consumer products. Digital natives, aka Millennials, are looking for genuine brands they can engage with, and Lily's creation story helps them understand what makes the Kangaroo Cup so unique. It's remarkable how important stories are to the Kickstarter products that succeed. Stories help create an emotional connection to a product, particularly with technology products where it's more often about sales than about the story. Too many companies forget about their story and focus instead only on sales numbers. The story is what drives the Kangaroo Brand. A lot of people forget that at the end of the day, we love stories.

Advice to Founders

In an ideal world, knowing what we know now, we should have gone for more distribution, and leveraged all of that great media exposure and broadcast around the world. If we'd had placement back then, we could have sold a lot more products. Kickstarter is too small a tool to build mass production. We wasted all the media exposure that we got and didn't get the most out of the publicity. We should have pushed to get into places where they sell millions of products. Kickstarter and CNN Hero were great for exposure, but at that point, we should have looked for a strategic partner, whose brand aligned with our story. We didn't do that, and as a result, we couldn't scale.

> *Don't be afraid to ask for help. No matter how good your idea is, there are lots of things that grownups will have to help you with.*
>
> —**Lily Born**, from *The Kangaroo Cup* by Leva Tilindyte, European Social Entrepreneurship and Innovative Studies Institute, DOIT Europe

Epilogue

The Kangaroo Cup launched Imagiroo, LLC, the company that Joe and Lily Born established in 2014. The cup now comes in multiple colors and in unbreakable plastic, making it useful not only for people with mobility issues, but for anyone who wants a durable cup. It is carried by major retailers Amazon, Walmart, and Target and sold nationwide. Lily Born is Imagiroo's Chairwoman and Chief Invention Officer—and a Junior at Niles West High School in Chicago. As a pre-teen, she was listed as *Business Insider's* top 11-year-old in Tech, and Mochi's "25 game changers under 25." Lily has exhibited her Kangaroo Cup at the White House Science Fair, The White House Woman's Expo, The Smithsonian Museum of American History, and Chicago's Museum of Science and Industry and has been honored as a CNN Heroes "young wonder." She has appeared on CNN Headline News, *NBC Nightly News*, NPR's *Weekend Edition*, *Fast Company*, *Business Insider*, and internationally on UK *Daily Mail* and *The Telegraph*, and on Chicago News Channels, Tribune Crain's Chicago Business, WGN's morning news, and CBS 2 News. Lily Born has been recognized by A Mighty Girl and Amy Poehler's Smart Girls as an inspiration to girls to follow their passion and their dreams. A part of the company's profits goes to support STEM education for girls.

> *Lily is the face of the Kangaroo Cup and tells the story of how the product came to be and the story of herself to show how an introvert can grow into role model.*
>
> —**Joe Born**, COO, Imagiroo

THE ART OF STORYTELLING

We humans are wired to connect to, and to relate with, one another through stories. In a 2014 *Techcrunch* article, Kobie Fuller reminds us that stories also "connect us to places, products and brands and help us identify which brands we champion by substituting promotion with engagement." Thanks to social media, startups can drive customers by "leveraging human emotion through the art of storytelling." To be successful, founders must learn what drives early adopters to make purchasing decisions. Fuller notes that "creative, emotion-driven marketing enables any size company to drive product awareness with millions of consumers in real-time. These digital and social direct-to-consumer channels have replaced traditional advertising that once favored larger companies with big budgets."

> *A brand without a narrative*
> *is a brand without customers.*
>
> —Mingo Press

All good stories need a compelling arc, a villain (the problem), and a hero (the solution) as well as clarity of purpose to make sure that you are tapping into, as Fuller says, the "story button part of the brain." A well-told story helps a startup connect through emotion-driven marketing, which creates more authentic moments of customer engagement. A well-told story helps a startup connect through emotion-driven marketing, which creates more authentic moments of customer engagement. The best marketing uses both art (empathic listening to better understand consumer needs and wants) and science (research and data analysis to identify consumer trends). In a 2017 *Forbes* article, Forbes Council member Jenna Gross states simply that "art gives marketing impact; data gives it direction."

Simon Sinek is a leadership guru, author, and motivational speaker. He became a YouTube sensation with his 2009 TED Talk "How Great Leaders Inspire Action." His iconic Golden Circle diagram identified the three key steps in the sales process and why most companies have it backward. A typical sales call, says Sinek, starts with what the company does, as in "we

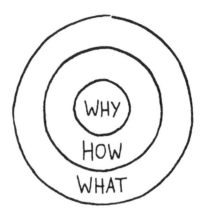

© 2017 Simon Sinek
from *Start With Why* by Simon Sinek

FIGURE 7.1
Simon Sinek's Golden Circle

make computers," and quickly moves into how they do it: "we use the latest technology and great design" and then they wait for the potential customer to buy their product. It turns out that people are much more motivated to buy an idea, which is why getting clear on your company's "why" is so critical to sales. When you can articulate why buying your product will change your customer's life for the better, competition falls away. Martin Luther King didn't have a plan, says Sinek. He had a dream. It's hard to imagine 250,000 people showing up to hear a plan (Figure 7.1).

CUSTOMER ENGAGEMENT

The most successful brands tap into the power of stories and use them to increase customer engagement. A great example is Airbnb.

In the second half of the 20th century, travel accommodations for the average American family were a hit-or-miss affair. Holiday Inn rose to brand leadership status in large part by taking the guesswork out of travel accommodations. It guaranteed that no matter where you traveled in the United States, your experience would be exactly the same.

Founded in 2008, Airbnb is a San Francisco company built on a diametrically opposed brand promise, based on the needs of a traveler who is looking for an immersive travel experience. There are two beneficiaries in an Airbnb experience: travelers, who gain a unique understanding of a place; and the locals, who become brand ambassadors for their town, their city, and their country.

Unlike the Holiday Inn franchise, Airbnb is not a brick-and-mortar company and sells no product. Instead, it curates content. Within a few years of its founding, it grew into a marketplace for people to list, discover, and book unique accommodations around the world. It now offers 600,000

8/10

major brands use stories.
(Rooted Web, 2019)

listings in 190 countries that includes 1,400+ castles and attracts 100,000 monthly users to their website and app. In 2017, Airbnb partnered with Hearst to create *AirbnbMag* to help travelers "see the world through a local lens." The stories and tips in the magazine (and digital edition) are hyperlocal, but also universal. Unlike a conventional travel magazine, *AirbnbMag* is more than just pretty pictures. It also depicts real-life stories from real people.

From a marketing perspective, Airbnb and *AirbnbMag* are using their customers' stories to sell their brand. It's a brilliant twist on traditional advertising and much more effective. We are far more likely to trust the stories of people who are sharing their personal travel experiences—both the good and the bad—than we are to trust a company's website to sell us on the benefits of immersive travel. This is what makes a magazine like *AirbnbMag* so effective. It provides authentic, curated content. The brand has come full circle.

I've learned that people will forget what you said, people will forget what you did, but people will never forget how you made them feel.

—**Maya Angelou**, author

GOOD STORIES BUILD GOOD BRANDS

Think of the last PowerPoint presentation you attended. What do you remember from it?

Maya Angelou famously said, "I've learned that people will forget what you said, people will forget what you did, but people will never forget how you made them feel." The average PowerPoint presentation isn't built around a story but instead favors facts and text-heavy slides that often leave listeners dazed and confused. In a 2017 CNBC *make it* article, Black Sheep founder Jeff Black notes that "leaders need to get back to being messengers instead of just reading off presentation slides" and that using the "power of a good story is the best way to influence others." Black also reminds us that "Steve Jobs … was the messenger, he was the star of the show—not the PowerPoint slide."

An estimated 33M PowerPoint presentations are given every day in the U.S. According to a 2018 Wall Street Journal *article, bad PowerPoint presentations cost companies $252 million/day in wasted time.*

—Tamayo Consulting

Jobs knew that complex ideas presented in a simple way were more likely to be remembered. Consequently, he typically used a one-sentence summary of a product to capture the main message he wanted to deliver. Shortly after launching the first iPhone in 2007, Jobs announced, "Apple reinvents the phone." It was the only sentence on

> **52%**
> of online brand discovery happens in public social media feeds.
> (Hootsuite, 2020)

the slide. To drive home the point during his presentation, he repeated the headline several times to make sure that people would remember it. A Google search for the phrase turns up roughly 25,000 links, most of which come directly from articles and blog posts covering the launch presentation.

Storytelling helps us connect with complex ideas and engage with brands on a personal level. As a result, we are more loyal to their products. Before launching a new product or service, startups should consider adding a story that ties it to a human experience. Stories not only build emotional connections but also make a startup more relatable and accessible to early adopters who will help build a community of brand evangelists.

We'll wrap up this chapter with an exercise to help you craft the perfect elevator pitch.

ELEVATOR PITCH EXERCISE

Note: an elevator pitch doesn't tell someone everything you do. It is not a sales pitch. An elevator pitch is meant to give someone just enough information to make them curious. You'll know you've succeeded when you hear: "Tell me more."

Before you start, outline your brand framework using a real-life example.

1. Outcome: one sentence that sums up what you do.
2. Tell a story of that outcome from one customer's perspective.
3. Identify one AHA moment.
4. Results—how your product/service changed your customer's life.

Now write one or two sentences that sum this up and is specific to the ideal customer you've identified in Chapter 3. If and only if they ask, you can share the story you outlined (be prepared to have more than one type of story so you can customize it to the person you're speaking to).

My elevator pitch is as follows: "I'm a brand architect. I help startups uncover their brand's DNA and close the marketing gaps that get in the way of scaling their business."

Be prepared. Your pitch will often fall flat. This is normal. Not everyone is a fit for what you offer. The right prospect will love your pitch and will want to learn more about your product, your company, and your brand.

8

The Future Is Entrepreneurial

*Entrepreneurship isn't a career choice,
it's a passion and obsession.*

—**Steve Blank**, father of modern entrepreneurship

Entrepreneurship is on the rise.

To understand this phenomenon, let's start with a major societal shift: the recession of 2008. The financial crisis of 2007 and the resulting recession of 2008 dramatically changed the way we think about work. As the number of displaced executives grew, many abandoned traditional job searches to launch new businesses and consulting practices. By 2010, roughly 8.7 million jobs were lost, and independent contractors grew in numbers and popularity. According to a 2018 *Forbes* magazine article, nearly 57 million U.S. workers have joined the gig economy, or more than one-third of the U.S. population.

Technology provides 24/7 real-time access to job searches and hiring talent. It has forever changed the way we work, play, and buy. Examples of this new reality are all around us: Craigslist launched in 1995 and is now in 70+ countries; Airbnb launched in 2008 and has grown to roughly 100,000 users on its site every month; Uber was founded in 2009, and the Uber app was launched in 2010.

The preoccupation with startups and their founders became a nationwide trend when the TV show *Shark Tank* premiered in the summer of 2009. Newly minted founders now had a global platform where the very notion of starting your company was celebrated and rewarded with lucrative investment partnerships. There are currently 400 million entrepreneurs worldwide.

> *If invention is a pebble tossed in the pond, innovation is the rippling effect that pebble causes. Someone has to toss the pebble. That's the inventor. Someone has to recognize the ripple will eventually become a wave. That's the entrepreneur.*
>
> —**Kim Bhasin**, *Business Insider*, 2012

It's not surprising that the popularity of starting your own business has given rise to entrepreneurship programs, from fewer than 200 in 1990 to more than 2,000 in 2014. There are currently 250 undergraduate degrees in entrepreneurship offered in the United States,[1] and the number is growing. More than 300 schools offer programs in entrepreneurship and for more than a decade, the *Princeton Review* has published a separate ranking for the top 25 undergraduate and top 25 graduate programs in entrepreneurship. The top-ranked Stanford Graduate Business School launched a Go-to-Market Program in 2015 for aspiring entrepreneurs and intrapreneurs to help them turn an idea into a business.

250

U.S. Bachelor Degrees in Entrepreneurship.
(Study Portals, 2020)

The popularity of entrepreneurship education has also helped spread the myth of the lone genius founder. A 2014 *Inc.* magazine article noted that even legendary loners like Steve Jobs and Jeff Bezos didn't go it alone. Yet the myth persists to this day, and the entrepreneurship students I've taught often have trouble overcoming it.

If you have an idea and something you want to pursue, this is a fantastic time in your life to try it. Just make sure you get as many successful business people as you can on your advisory board. We couldn't have done it without them. We needed their expertise to launch properly.

—**RJ Napolitano**, founder, Zebra

I've found that there are three key components to building a student startup that can go beyond school walls and succeed in the real world.

- Building the right team and the right culture
- Identifying the right product/service for the right customer
- Working with a seasoned team of advisors

STUDENT FOUNDER: ETHAN BRESNAHAN, BOOST LINGUISTICS

Boost Linguistics won first place at Drexel University, Baiada Institute Business Model Competition in 2015. Ethan readily admits that he wished he'd let go of the myth of the genius loner sooner and focused instead on building a startup culture and growing the right team.

As a founder, you wear many hats, and at first, that kind of flexibility can be an asset. But as time goes by, the lone genius myth can make students feel uncomfortable about letting go of their own ideas and turn to seasoned experts for advice. Some see it as a sign of weakness to admit that they don't have all the answers.

You have to be honest with yourself and acknowledge what you're good at and what challenges you. You can't outsource what you don't want to do, so you have to learn on the job and you have to do it fast!

I wish I'd focused on building a startup culture and growing the right team. I discovered that friends are not always a good fit, and that created tensions when we tried to scale. I had to learn how to have difficult conversations and let people go who weren't aligned with our vision.

Developers have a sandbox and all the time to play. As a student, it's even more important to have an entrepreneurial sandbox. Stakes are relatively low, and it's easier to get seed money. Investors like the PR that comes from giving funding to students, and that was their motivation to invest in our company. You have to capitalize on being a student and being new. Find people quickly who want to invest in you as an individual before they invest in your company. Advisors told me that believing in the founder was primary. If they believe in you, they will support you as an individual and whatever it is you're doing.

Find what you're good at. I found out that I'm really good at PR. I was the face of the company and became known as the "Boost Guy."

—**Ethan Bresnahan**, co-founder, Boost Linguistics

You're not a failure if you walk away. Failure hurts, but it's a great learning experience, and I didn't walk away from entrepreneurship. I joined a small team at another startup, Post series A, so I get to see the full arc. It's unusual to hit it out of the park the way that Mark Zuckerberg did. What I realized is that just because Boost didn't work out, I still got a lot of positive feedback from mentors who saw something in me. When I told my advisors that I was leaving, one of my mentors said "Thank goodness you realized it because someone would have had to say something." That same mentor told me to call him when I start my next thing because he wants to be part of that too.

Epilogue

Boost Linguistics was featured in a 2017 *Inc.* article on student entrepreneurs and was one of the companies presented at the 2017 SXSW trade show. The company closed in 2018 and Ethan is now a brand and marketing manager at CyberSaint, a cyber security startup in Boston. In 2019, he was approached by a company interested in purchasing the technology that Ethan and his co-founders developed for Boost Linguistics.

THE LONE GENIUS MYTH

It's easy to understand why college students have elevated founders like Elon Musk and Mark Zuckerberg to myth status. After all, what is more alluring to an aspiring entrepreneur than the idea of a lone genius (and Harvard dropout) who changed the fabric of social discourse and created a new way of communication, with only his drive and imagination to guide him. Students, along with the rest of us, love to romanticize the quirky outliers with a burning desire to change the world. But the myth of the lone genius is just that, a myth. The reality is much less glamorous but also more realistic and much more attainable.

It is true that Zuckerberg created something extraordinary, but Facebook as we know it today took years of hard work from a lot of people who believed in his vision and were willing to sacrifice short-term gains for long-term benefits. The lone genius is often the catalyst for a great idea, but you need the right team to help make your vision a reality. In the case of Facebook, it included designers, developers, business advisors, seasoned executives, and investors.

Ethan Bresnahan believes that the lone genius myth may have its roots in comic book superheroes. Just as our favorite hero saved the day, we like the simplicity of the lone genius narrative in the business world. It makes for a great story, but the reality is that a startup is a complex ecosystem with many unsung heroes. The lone genius myth may also create barriers to scaling.

I found that many of my students in the Close School of Entrepreneurship at Drexel University focused much of their creative energy on trying to come up with something no one had ever done before, to be the first. As a result, they often missed the opportunity to improve on customer experience for existing products. Not everything needs to be built from the ground up. It's time-consuming and expensive. Carving out a niche in a known and lucrative market is a lofty goal and a smart business model. If you put aside ego, you can look for those opportunities and still be a successful entrepreneur.

Storytelling can serve as a good framework when talking about building a student startup. How does your origin story play a role in identifying who you are? Your ideal customer? How does your story engage that customer and the people who identify with that story and will want to invest in you to see your vision realized? That's

27/100

U.S. employees quit their jobs in 2018 or 41.4 million.
(PeopleKeep.com, 2018)

why the first step to building your brand should be to identify your vision. If you don't, how do you build an authentic story? Student founders rarely take the time to identify and communicate their vision, and as a result they spend a lot of time throwing things on the wall to see what sticks. The lack of vision hurts them when it comes to building a successful team and this has a direct impact on their bottom line. As I mentioned in Chapter 1, having the wrong team is the #3 reason that startups fail.

Teaching in the Close School showed me that not everyone is cut out to be an entrepreneur. That's a good thing to discover while you're still in your 20s. I believe that the true value of entrepreneurship education may lie in how students learn to adapt to the future of work. They become strategic thinkers who can pivot without missing a beat, and let go of ideas that don't work, in favor of products that customers truly need, want, and will pay for.

The illiterate of the 21st Century will not be those who cannot read and write, but those who cannot learn, unlearn and relearn.

—**Alvin Toffler**, noted futurist and author, *Future Shock*

In his 1970 book *Future Shock*, the noted futurist and author Alvin Toffler anticipated the rapid rate of change that technology would have on modern life. We began to feel its impact when the second industrial revolution ushered in the age of personal computers and again, more profoundly, during the third industrial revolution, which brought us the Internet. We are now in a perpetual state of change as better, faster, and ever-more-complex technology alters the way we communicate, work, and live.

| 20+M |
| Estimated number of jobs worldwide to be replaced by robots by 2030. (Oxford Economics Study, 2019) |

Toffler's iconic phrase "today is the least amount of change you'll see in your lifetime" rings especially true as we enter the fourth industrial revolution and with it, artificial intelligence, augmented reality, and machine learning. As robots begin to replace jobs traditionally done by humans, Toffler's other prediction is proving to be true as well—that the very idea of a job would become obsolete and that lifelong learning was the future.

As we grapple with the new realities of the fourth industrial revolution, entrepreneurial thinking could provide a blueprint to help us navigate the impact of perpetual change in our personal and professional lives.

NOTE

1 https://www.bachelorsportal.com/study-options/269779030/entrepreneurship-united-states.html

9

Conclusion

Show Me the Money

> *The world is rapidly moving from marketing as a cost,*
> *to marketing as a revenue driver.*

—**Edward Nevraumont**, author, *Marketing B.S.*

Marketing is the engine that runs sales. It identifies qualified leads and reminds consumers why they would want to buy your product. Sales takes those qualified leads and tries to convert them into customers. Together, sales and marketing help turn a consumer into a customer.

Before the World Wide Web brought the world to us, marketing dollars were spent primarily on advertising to seduce consumers with promises of a better life, if only you used the right kind of toothpaste or drove the right car. Sales brochures were printed by the millions and traditional advertising was king—TV and radio commercials filled the airwaves and billboards littered our roads and highways; magazine and newspapers ads became part of a rising consumer culture.

Eventually, consumers began to view advertising as a means to convince them to buy things they didn't really need. They questioned the advertising—and eventually, many of them dismissed it. ROI diminished, and business owners began to think of marketing as something akin to "smoke and mirrors." This led to a new paradigm that marketing was unnecessary and a waste of money. Consequently, whenever the economy took a sharp turn downward, companies slashed their marketing budgets to reduce expenses. This is a costly mistake. According to a 2019 *Forbes* article, when you invest in marketing during a slowdown, you're ensuring that you'll be ready for the upturn.[1]

When some brands cut back on their marketing dollars, it's easier for others to cut through the noise and stand out when they stay the course. Downturns are also a great time to invest in innovation and introduce new products. When companies resist the urge to slash marketing budgets, they project an image of corporate stability. Most important, cutting your marketing dollars can result in lost market share in the mind of consumers and the potential to lose current and future sales. As we all know, an increase in market share means an increase in profits.[2]

One example of a company that emerged stronger after the recession of 2008 is Amazon. Instead of slashing their marketing budget, Amazon invested those dollars in R&D to come up with new Kindle products and grow their market share. On Christmas Day 2009, Amazon customers bought more e-books than printed books. In the minds of consumers, Amazon became an innovative company by introducing a lower-cost alternative to cash-strapped consumers. As a result, Amazon sales grew by 28% during the great recession.[3]

In a 2009 *Harvard Business Review* article, John Quelch, the Charles Edward Wilson professor of Business Administration Emeritus at Harvard, cautions that "Successful companies do not abandon their marketing strategies in a recession; they adapt them."[4]

Marketing should not be relegated to an item on your balance sheet; it's the engine that keeps your business going. The thing about an engine is that you have to keep fueling it, or it dies. For a startup, investing in marketing from the start is critical to scaling and growth. As we have already discovered, traditional marketing is not effective for a startup, but that doesn't mean that they shouldn't invest in marketing at all. Lean Marketing helps founders identify their ideal customer, hone in on their brand messaging, and attract early adopters. It's important to remember that when startups limit their marketing budget to a small sliver of their overall spending pie, their business stays the same size, and so does their marketing budget. Conversely, when founders invest a larger portion of that pie in marketing, their business grows exponentially, providing more money for marketing and future growth.

LEAN MARKETING

In today's digital age, marketing has evolved into a shared experience that is focused primarily on content marketing and includes videos, blogs, white papers, and social media feeds. Social media has emerged as a powerful tool for startups. With the right content, founders can engage with their early adopters and build buzz for their nascent company. And for the most part, it's free, which is good news since startups can't compete with established brands through traditional marketing buys. Social media statistics are so compelling that they bear repeating. In 2019, Facebook users generated 4 million likes every minute, Twitter users uploaded 6,000 tweets every second, and more than 95 million photos were posted on Instagram every day. Consumers trust the opinions of influencers, so it's good business to get to know the influencers in your industry as a first step to building buzz for your startup. Engaging with those influencers regularly means that their followers (typically in the millions) will learn about your brand. It's a great alternative to expensive social media buys (Figure 9.1).

Remember that social media is a numbers game. Building your brand there is an investment of time, but one worth making. As the founder, you are the face of your startup, so before you run out and get an intern to manage your social media feeds, make sure you have a cohesive social media strategy in place—one that is based on a deep understanding of your target market and what matters to them. It's not just content, for content's sake. The 80/20 rule works well here: 80% of the content you post should be focused—on industry stats, quotes, or trends, for example. The remaining 20% should be sales focused—news about developments at your startup, for example, or a speaking invitation at a national conference, or a new product launch. Make it your priority to create daily content that your intern can share. A note of caution: if you want to see results you'll need to post one to two times a day on Facebook and Instagram, five to ten times a day on Twitter, and once per business day on LinkedIn. Luckily, there are software programs that can send out content for you at designated times. Once you've grown your social media presence to multiple platforms, you'll want to explore those options.

FIGURE 9.1
Content Marketing Strategy Map

The most successful brands offer customized content that is not only relevant to their customers but is also aligned with their core values and the products and services they offer. The good news for startups is that with the right content strategy, they can multiply the value of their marketing dollars.

MARKETING ROI

In our bottom-line-focused culture, CEOs are impatient to see immediate returns on their marketing dollars. They often expect their CMO to take a modest marketing budget and magically turn it into new customer sales and healthy revenue. But marketing is not the same thing as selling. It's not simply about deducting the cost of goods sold (COGS) from the selling price and spitting out a profit. Marketing ROI does not live on a balance sheet like sales do. Marketing is an investment that a company makes in its future growth and success.

In a 2020 article, Andrew Beattie, former managing editor and longtime contributor at Investopedia.com explains it this way: "Marketing is everything a company does to acquire customers and maintain a relationship with them."[5] Companies that see marketing as an investment focus on long-term goals and metrics, not short-term gains or losses.

> *Content Marketing is a commitment, not a campaign.*
> —**Michael Brenner**, CEO, Marketing Insider Group

MEASURING MARKETING ROI

In the same article, Beattie says that the easiest way to measure the ROI of marketing is to take the sales growth from your business or product line, subtract the marketing costs, and then divide by the marketing cost.

Sales Growth – Marketing Cost/Marketing Cost = ROI

So, if sales grew by $1,000 and the marketing campaign cost $100, then the simple ROI is 900%.

($1,000 – $100) / $100 = 900%

Another ROI that CEOs rarely consider is the impact that marketing can have on slowing down negative sales growth. If sales have been dropping on average of $1,000 a month, and a $500 marketing campaign results in a sales drop of only $200 that month, then the ROI is the $800 ($1,000 – $200) you avoided losing. So even though sales dropped, your campaign has an ROI of 60%.[6]

($800 – $500) / $500 = 60%

ROI may be flat or low as the campaign starts to gain traction, but as time goes by, sales growth should follow and the cumulative ROI of the campaign will start to improve. If after six months, there is no uptick in sales, then a review of your marketing strategy is in order.

In a 2016 interview on the podcast *B2B Nation*, Marketing Insider CEO Michael Brenner explains content marketing ROI this way: "Committing yourself to building a content brand is like building a retirement account. If you put money into a retirement account, it might not look like much in a year. But after five years, you start to see the impact of the investment. Content marketing works the same way. When you track the results, you start to see compounding rates of return. If you publish an article two or three times a week, and you do that for 52 weeks, what happens is that there's an accelerating increase. The first article you publish is still getting page views a year later. It's gaining reach to an audience."[7]

Marketing is a marathon, not a sprint. That's why a marketing strategy is critical to long-term growth and success. Ask yourself:

- What are you hoping to achieve?
- Are you looking to build brand awareness for your new startup?
- Is it about increasing market penetration and growing sales?
- Are you building the case for an acquisition or getting ready to take your company public?

If you can't answer these questions, you'll be throwing things on a wall to see what sticks. And that's expensive and ineffective.

Traditional marketing is not dead, but it's out of the reach of the average startup and won't help founders establish a competitive advantage. Traditional marketing is a much better fit for well-established brands with deep pockets. Startup founders should reconsider the goal of marketing as a 30-second Super Bowl spot. In 2019, that 30-second buy cost more than $5 million. That's the reason it's reserved for brands like Apple and Nike to help them maintain their leadership status. Startup marketing should focus instead on building brand awareness and growing social media followers. Social media helps brands stay current on industry trends and keeps their content relevant to their customers. It also helps measure engagement, build buzz, and turn customers into brand ambassadors.

Instead of waiting until they've built an advertising arsenal, startup founders should be building a content strategy. The first step is to follow the social media feeds of leading brands over a three-month period to learn how they engage with their customers and what content resonates with those customers. Remember that the proof is in the numbers. If your company has fewer than 200 followers on any social media platform, it's time to re-evaluate your content.

Resist the impulse to change course too soon. Multiple and inconsistent marketing campaigns can negatively impact your company and make you look indecisive and disjointed. In the long run, a short-term approach to marketing can hurt your brand image and make it harder to build brand loyalty, and that's bad for business.

THE BOTTOM LINE ON LEAN MARKETING

In 2019, more than 50% of U.S. startups failed after four years. And only three in ten survive the 10-year mark.[8]

I believe that the Lean Marketing principles I've covered in this book can make a real difference in the lifespan of a startup.

By now, I hope you've come to see that marketing is more than smoke and mirrors and that the time to start branding and marketing is now. If you wait for the right time, you'll never get to it.

I also hope I've shattered a few myths, from "we get all our business from referrals" to "a website is nice to have but not critical" to "great products sell themselves." And, that you come away from reading this book with an appreciation not only of the power of social media to fuel your startup, but the importance of finding your own voice and being true to your core value.

Along the way, we've heard from a number of founders who have experienced the highs—and lows—of entrepreneurship in the modern age. May their experiences inform and inspire you on your startup journey.

Ready, Launch, Brand.

NOTES

1 https://www.forbes.com/sites/bradadgate/2019/09/05/when-a-recession-comes-dont-stop-advertising/#596936414608
2 https://www.forbes.com/sites/bradadgate/2019/09/05/when-a-recession-comes-dont-stop-advertising/#596936414608
3 https://www.forbes.com/sites/bradadgate/2019/09/05/when-a-recession-comes-dont-stop-advertising/#596936414608
4 https://hbr.org/2008/09/how-to-market-in-a-recession
5 https://www.investopedia.com/articles/personal-finance/053015/how-calculate-roi-marketing-campaign.asp
6 https://www.investopedia.com/articles/personal-finance/053015/how-calculate-roi-marketing-campaign.asp
7 https://technologyadvice.com/blog/marketing/michael-brenner-content-marketing-is-a-commitment-not-a-campaign/
8 https://www.smallbizgenius.net/by-the-numbers/startup-statistics/#gref

Index

Page numbers in *italic* indicate figures.

For Product Safety Concerns and Information please contact our EU
representative GPSR@taylorandfrancis.com
Taylor & Francis Verlag GmbH, Kaufingerstraße 24, 80331 München, Germany

www.ingramcontent.com/pod-product-compliance
Ingram Content Group UK Ltd.
Pitfield, Milton Keynes, MK11 3LW, UK
UKHW020931180425
457613UK00012B/313